Next-Level Content Marketing

Next-Level Content Marketing

Advanced Tactics for Today's Content Marketer

By Ted Box

with Kathryn Aragon

Zug, Switzerland

BOXONLINE
Bahnhofstr 23
CH-6300 Zug
Switzerland

Copyright © Ted Box, 2014

All rights reserved. No part of this book may be reproduced, scanned, or distributed in any printed or electronic form without written permission. Please do not participate in or encourage piracy of copyrighted materials in violation of the author's rights. Purchase only authorized editions.

Every effort has been made to make this book as complete and as accurate as possible, but no warranty or fitness is implied. The information provided is on an "as is" basis. The author and the publisher shall have neither liability nor responsibility to any person or entity with respect to any loss or damages arising from the information contained in this book.

Dedication

Dedicated to leading marketers,
without whom none of this would be possible.
Thank you for breaking out of the shackles of mediocrity
and taking action to be remarkable.

Contents

Foreword	iii
Introduction	ix
Chapter 1: Content Is King-ish	1
Chapter 2: How to Create Magnetic Content	25
Chapter 3: Improving Content Delivery	57
Chapter 4: Repeating and Improving the Cycle	85
Chapter 5: Growing Your List	115
Chapter 6: Advanced Content Strategies	135
Conclusion: The Key is Engagement	179
Appendix	185
About the Author	193

Foreword

We are flooded with information now. Deluged with it. Time lines, video feeds, transactions, sensor data, infographics, CRM, GPS, whatever—we've all seen the numbers. So many gigabytes of data generated every few seconds on Facebook, so many years' worth of video uploaded every hour to YouTube, more new information created every few days than was generated from the beginning of history up through the year 2003.

But as Herbert Simon once said, "A wealth of information creates a poverty of attention." And that's the big challenge for today's content marketer, because the amount of human attention span in the world is relatively fixed, while the demand for it continues to soar, as everyone becomes a publisher and all the world is an increasingly over-marketed audience.

If you're a marketer, then now is the time to think more clearly about the purpose, usefulness, and effectiveness of your content—which is to say, the purpose, usefulness, and effectiveness of your marketing. And that's the issue Ted Box addresses in *Next-Level Content Marketing*.

Some marketers, judging by their campaigns, apparently think that the objective of content marketing is simply to find better ways to push their sales pitches out to more ears, more frequently and voluminously than the competition. But as the tide of data from everywhere continues to surge, higher and higher, reaching those ears becomes that much more difficult, so their marketing hamster wheels just spin faster and faster, and they still don't get there.

On the other hand, if you share my own belief that the purpose of content marketing isn't to broadcast your

sales pitch 24/7, but to provide your prospects and customers with useful, entertaining, or interesting information designed to help them solve the problems they're trying to solve or meet the needs they're trying to meet, then this is just the book for you.

I think the best possible kind of marketing for almost any business, over the long term, involves trying to act in the customer's own interest at all times. This doesn't mean giving the product away at a loss or providing costly services that can't be paid for. What it means is simply understanding the need that an individual customer wants met, and then trying to help that customer meet that need, in the same way *you* would want to be helped, if *you* were that customer.

This kind of marketing is truly customer-focused. It should transcend product and brand silos in order to treat different customers differently, integrating everything your business is capable of doing on behalf of each individual customer. It should be based on each customer's previous interactions and signals—all the data that an individual customer throws off during the process of finding, buying, and using your product, or consuming your helpful information.

This is the kind of marketing that's designed to sell, not by overwhelming the customer with persuasiveness, but by engaging the customer in a collaborative interaction. It's almost not fair to call it "marketing," because what you should really be trying to do with your content is *give* it to the customer in order to *help*. If you do it right, you will (1) demonstrate that you have useful expertise and advice, and (2) predispose the customer to want to repay that helpful advice.

In the final analysis, engaging customers with your content should be equivalent to engaging them with your business—your brand, your product, your reason for being.

But even if you do have the correct mindset with respect to using content marketing to make yourself indispensable to customers and prospects, you will still need to figure out how to be sure that these customers and prospects can actually find out about it. And that their curiosity will be aroused enough that they will want to explore it on their own.

This, also, is a topic explored in *Next-Level Content Marketing*. In the e-social era, the customer can no longer be treated as a target, or as some anonymous "recipient" of your outbound messaging. If you run a smart business, you will think of the customer as your ally. Your collaborator. Your friend. And you should be trying to help your friend solve his problem by using your content.

So it goes without saying, your content, standing completely on its own, needs to have genuine value—that is, that your potential customer should find it useful, entertaining, or informative whether or not they ever buy from you.

But then you need to add some sizzle to that steak, so stay tuned to get a few juicy cooking tips!

Don Peppers

Don Peppers is one of the world's most recognized experts on customer-centric business strategies. Founding Partner at Peppers & Rogers Group, his most recent book, with Martha Rogers, is *Extreme Trust: Honesty as a Competitive Advantage.*

Introduction

Think of a salesperson who walks up to you in a store. "Thanks, I'm okay, I'm just looking," you tell him. But he hovers and looms, finds ways to insert himself into your activity, and is a general annoyance. In theory, even if that salesperson had something meaningful to say, the method of delivery erased the value of the content. You might even walk out of the store.

That's what most marketing feels like: intrusive and unwelcome. Engagement Marketing is the opposite. It's a salesperson who hangs back and engages with you if and when you need help. This is the salesperson who can sense what you want to do and will help you arrive at that final decision to buy, who will contact you directly with exclusive sales information, if—and only if—you request it.

When you liken it to a shopping experience, it makes sense. Why, then, is it so hard for us to see this when we're hard at work in the marketing department? The traditional high-volume, low-percentage communication approach is inherently flawed. Most of us don't want constant contact. We don't enjoy being interrupted. We don't even want it from our best friends, let alone a large, faceless company we barely know.

Engagement marketing done well, however, means connecting with people who want to hear from you in relevant, meaningful, interesting ways. And especially, at the moment they need the information you provide. If you can pull that off, everything changes.

But content today isn't actually doing this.

In theory, content marketing is the solution we marketers are looking for. It has all the potential of being a low-pressure way to connect with, and build relationships with, our audience, developing trust and leading people gently into the sales funnel. But for many businesses—even businesses that are doing content marketing correctly—this isn't actually happening.

The concept is right. So what's wrong?

Two things. First, getting our content in front of our ideal audience is a bigger challenge than ever before. And second, when we do get it in front of them, we struggle to keep their attention. Unless we can overcome these two obstacles, we can't gain all the benefits content marketing promises.

You see, there are two sides to the content marketing coin. On one side is *content creation*. You must be able to create messages that your audience sees as valuable and engaging. That's where most content marketers spend their energy.

But there's another side to the coin, and that is *content delivery*. Unfortunately, this side of the issue is rarely explored. And it's where most content marketing falls short. In a digital world that is gaining new ways of engaging and talking to one another each and every day, we're still delivering content the same way we did ten years ago or more.

We publish blog posts on our websites, and videos, audios, messages and SlideShares on all sorts of other sites. We can embed that media in our blog posts (isn't technology grand?) and use email and social media to let people know there's something they need to look at. That's all good, and it's working relatively well for those with a following. Each day, however, we find new solutions for integrating it all. It's moving *forward*. It's evolving at an exponential pace.

Now let's look at our high-value content: our brochures, eBooks, special reports, catalogs, newsletters, brand magazines, etc. We publish them—if not in print—in PDF format, quickly becoming one of the most outdated formats available in our digital, social world. Some brands are moving to flipbooks. Good for them. But a flipbook is just a PDF with page-flipping distractions. With all the technology at our fingertips, you'd think we could come up with something better!

Actually, there is something better, but we'll talk about that later. Right now, what I want to call out is the need for content delivery to get the same focus as content creation.

It's the other side (the often forgotten side) of content marketing. And it may have greater potential to engage and delight your audience than the content itself. Neglect it at your own peril.

This is what keeps most marketers from taking their content to the next level. They leave off one or more of the elements that make content the king of Engagement Marketing: truly magnetic content, a delivery platform that makes full use of technology, or an optimization process after the content goes live. In this book, we'll explore each of these areas. We're going to dive deep. This is not a beginner's guide to content marketing; rather, it's an attempt to move successful content marketers to the next level, a place I like to call 'the zone.' If you are ready for the challenge, welcome aboard. We're about to embark on a journey into the largely uncharted territory of advanced content marketing.

Chapter 1

Content Is King-ish

It became a cliché to say content is king, mostly because it's true. Or at least true-ish. Content, if not delivered effectively, leaves the king powerless. (Remember the annoying salesperson in the store?)

Picture this: you are one of the nearly 200 million drivers in the United States. You are driving from point A to point B, and all you can think about it what to feed your kids when you get home. You are quickly approaching a billboard for a local fast food restaurant—but you drive right past it, not even giving it a look.

Ironically, you're too focused on what to feed your family to see the solution—even when one is right in front of you.

Soon, however, you approach another billboard, which advertises a competitor to the first one. The difference is that this one catches your attention. It offers a quick solution to your problem, so you get off at the next exit and grab some dinner.

What was the difference? You *saw* the second billboard.

Why did it catch your attention when the first billboard failed to do so? The first billboard was your everyday, run-of-the-mill static billboard with an image and logo. Because you see them so often, you've developed billboard blindness. They are simply a part of the landscape. The second billboard, however, was a digital billboard. It flashed, was animated, and switched from one advertisement to another. It stood out from all other billboards, so you were able to see it. And once you saw it, you could see the message as well.

Now, what are we talking about here? We are talking about engagement. Today, you're bombarded with three hundred to six thousand marketing messages a day, according to Terry O'Reilly and Mike Tennant, in *The Age of Persuasion*. You see them everywhere: in your inbox, in your social media streams, on billboards, in magazines, everywhere from the bulletin board at the office to the subway walls. As humans, we can't process that much information and still function in an effective way. So we've become adept at filtering the information that comes at us, quickly skimming and scanning to identify what's relevant and what's important—then ignoring the rest.

Inevitably, much of the marketing we see falls into the "ignore" category. It isn't relevant, much less important. And in most cases, that decision is made in seconds, because marketing is so easily identified as useless or repetitive. The marketing that gets noticed has several key elements. It's engaging. It's different. It addresses something that matters to your audience.

Like that billboard, it targets the need—food for a hungry family—but in a way that it stands out and breaks through the clutter. When it does that, marketing becomes useful, and it often is internalized, remembered, and even shared with others.

Grabbing your Audience's Attention

The difference between marketing that gets ignored and marketing that is seen and responded to is simple: one is static while the other is dynamic. What is dynamic marketing? It is content and collateral that leverages all the power of technology now available on the social Web. Instead of a static PDF, it allows pages to flip or slide. Instead of flat graphics, it employs kinetic animations, audio, video or other media. Dynamic marketing is up-to-date, interactive, and sharable, so it's appropriate for consumers who are plugged in and connected 24/7.

By the way, there's a word for flat, boring content. Click here to see what it is: http://123.ch/boringcontent.

(This link takes you to one page in a brochure. Does your content allow you to create a link to an internal page?) My goal in writing this book is to present a cure for content that lulls your readers to sleep rather than engaging and building loyalty. This book is a diagnosis and prescription for static, ineffective content. It is a challenge to all content creators to take content marketing to a new level.

Two, maybe three years ago, you could get away with static marketing. The social Web hadn't infiltrated society to the degree it has now. Today, if you aren't leveraging the full power of social media and the Web, you're falling behind.

If you're a business owner or marketer who is still using static marketing, you are probably seeing declines in response, year against year. Your story isn't getting any further than your audiences' inbox, which means it isn't getting read, isn't being shared, and isn't bringing you money. Grabbing the attention of today's "reader" requires that you digitize your story and make it stand out from everything else competing for attention. Take it from the PDF to the electronic device. Or take that flat, print brochure, and turn it into an immersive digital experience that potential customers *want* to read.

Why waste your time and money marketing your business using antiquated delivery formats? Junk mail, newspapers, and catalogs are in a death spiral. (Yes, they worked fine in 2007. Get over it.) Turn your marketing materials into digital images, animations, videos, podcasts, eZines, tweets, and Facebook posts. Create digital billboards drivers will actually notice, bestsellers your audience will read. We now work and operate in the Connection Age. Create something worth connecting to.

In the Connection Age, Engagement Is Everything

The Connection Age is about more than simply sharing information. It's about being connected to people all over the world from the moment we open our eyes in the morning to the time we turn out the light at night.

The degree of connection we have today is like nothing the world has ever experienced. We can work and play with people anywhere on the planet. We can hold meetings in real time, instant message, and share links with someone on another continent, just as if we were sitting across from one another in a conference room. Five years ago, you might be invited to a meeting at two o'clock. Today your first thought is to ask what time zone that is, because you could be meeting with someone five to ten time zones away.

In the Connection Age, geography and time are no longer limiting factors. As a result, we have much more input to contend with. I review my Facebook wall and see posts in German, Japanese, Swedish, and French, as well as in English. I see posts about multiple religions and different political views. I'm no longer isolated by geography, so I'm exposed to all ways of thinking and viewing the world. You and your audience are the same. Few people only see information that perfectly aligns with their own viewpoints.

As a marketer, this is the stage you perform on. It is colorful and busy. By comparison, static marketing is like that plain billboard, destined to be ignored. Sandwiched between a meme from someone's best friend and a video of kittens playing clarinets, it fails to register on readers' radar.

The competition is fierce, my friend. The only way you can survive is to learn how to engage people on a totally new level.

Start with Emotion

According to research by Gallup, "Emotionally satisfied customers deliver significantly enhanced value to an organization…[they do this] by buying more products, spending more for those products, returning more often, and staying longer with the business." What does that mean? It means that evoking emotions in your marketing works immediately, driving engagement and sales, and for the long term, breeding branding loyalty that keeps customers coming back for more.

Behavioral economists have suggested that people buy for rational reasons only 30 percent of the time. The majority of the time (70 percent), we buy for emotional reasons. Yet ironically, most marketing, if it doesn't resort to hype, doesn't engage emotionally. Often, it is stripped of emotion, relying on facts and logic to sway consumers. Frankly, this type of marketing uses the wrong tool and aims at the wrong target.

Only through emotions can you effectively engage your audience. The challenge, then, is two-fold: first, to be able to arouse emotions without appearing manipulative, and, second, to know which emotions are most effective to engage your particular audience. Interestingly, two emotions stand out from all others. Studies on video ads found that joy and surprise are especially effective at engaging viewers, with surprise improving attention, and joy improving retention of the ad's message. Yet any emotion can be effective, as long as it improves engagement levels.

For instance, negative emotions such as sadness, disgust, anger, or fear, are often used to drive people away from an action. This works best when people feel their personal interests are at stake, which is why this approach is so often used in financial and political marketing.

One of the first examples that comes to mind is a 1970s American advertisement discouraging pollution. It opens with a native American canoeing through pristine waters. Soon the water becomes filthy with bits of trash and industrial waste. The Indian pulls his canoe onto a polluted shore and stands next to a busy, smoggy highway. Trash, thrown out of a passing car, lands at his feet, and the camera zooms in. Now we see it—the single, sorrow-filled tear drop on his cheek, and we connect with his pain. (You can view the commercial on YouTube at http://123.ch/negativeemotion.)

The message was loud and clear. America the Beautiful cannot exist unless pollution ends. It was a public message intended to stop a negative action, pollution. And it worked. Based on that ad, pollution was no longer tolerated by the general population. An emotionally packed ad was all it took to unite people around an issue. Of course, you can just as easily drive action with a positive emotion tapping into joy, love, curiosity, wonder, and kindness.

For example, a Pfizer commercial shows a teen prowling the city streets at night. We watch as he paints graffiti on the side of a building then skulks home. As he enters the apartment, you get the idea that he's been in trouble before. His mother looks worried and rolls her eyes as she glances at her watch. Meanwhile, the boy grabs some flowers from a vase and disappears into the back of the apartment. He places the flowers beside a young girl's hospital bed and opens the bedroom's curtains. As viewers, we now begin to understand. The child, his sister, sits up in bed. The mother walks in and they all look out the window. The mother glances at her son again, but this time she mouths the words, "Thank you." Now, at last, the camera spins and we see as well. On the walls across from their apartment, the boy has spray-painted an encouraging message to his sister: Be brave. (View this commercial on YouTube at http://123.ch/positiveemotion.)

This ad easily brings a tear to your eye. It never mentions a product or appears to drive action. Its sole purpose seems to be public relations, to generate a positive brand perception. The message? That Pfizer is working to help people like you and me.

As you can see, by evoking emotions, you can drive brand perception or action, and get your words read or your videos watched. That's the power of emotion. It engages and keeps us engaged. And it's a powerful tool for developing brand loyalty, especially if you evoke positive emotions in your marketing.

We're Wired for Stories

Since cave-man days, people have been telling stories. We see stories of The Hunt on cave walls in France. We have Greek epics, *The Iliad* and *The Odyssey*, which began as oral stories spun by Homer in the Bronze Age. In more recent years, we've moved to novels, pulp fiction, and magazine articles. And most recently, thanks to the Internet, we also have blog posts, micro blogs, and memes.

These are all forms of storytelling. And we love them. Which is why you've been hearing for some time that content is king.

It was in 2009 that the phrase began to be batted around the marketing department. Up until that point, content was being developed, but it hadn't become a specific marketing task. Joe Pulizzi was one of the first content marketing advocates, and his teachings quickly caught on. Interestingly, it wasn't Joe who coined the phrase, *content is king*. That honor goes to Bill Gates, in an essay he wrote in 1996.

This ground-breaking essay was an incredibly accurate forecast of where the Internet would go. In it, Gates proclaimed,

> "Content is where I expect much of the real money will be made on the Internet, just as it was in broadcasting."

He was primarily focusing on the cost of publishing. But read this:

> "To be successful online, a magazine can't just take what it has in print and move it to the electronic realm. There isn't enough depth or interactivity in print content to overcome the drawbacks of the online medium.

> "If people are to be expected to put up with turning on a computer to read a screen, they must be rewarded with deep and extremely up-to-date

information that they can explore at will. They need to have audio, and possibly video. They need an opportunity for personal involvement that goes far beyond that offered through the letters-to-the-editor pages of print magazines."

Who would have guessed in 1996 that "content marketing" would actually become a "thing"? Since then, it's been iterated (*ad nauseum*) that content is king and that content, by definition, is broader than merely words on a page. Content is audio, video, and SlideShares as well. Today, it includes tweets, Facebook posts, and pins. Just as Bill Gates said, nearly 20 years ago, content creators are looking for ways to give people an opportunity to get personally involved.

The difference today is that "turning on a computer" isn't as novel nor does it take as long as it did in 1996. We don't need extra incentive to turn on a digital device; we've built that into our schedules already. Today, people don't care whether content comes to them on a television, radio, computer or phone. What matters is that it is interesting.

That's where story comes in. Not only do stories engage people emotionally, they create a framework for people to remember your message. As content creators, we aren't just marketers. We're also journalists, looking for a story to tell. Because people love a compelling story.

The New Consumer

We've already talked about how today's consumer is plugged in and social. What we haven't talked about is how that has changed consumer expectations.

Consumers don't trust advertising or what brands say about themselves. Ironically, they do trust content, as long as it isn't obviously self-promotional. They also trust their peers' recommendations in social media.

Interestingly, brands can become trusted friends, if they're willing to engage with people through social channels. What's more, consumers have begun to expect this. When people interact with a brand, they expect it to be a favorable experience. If it is, they share it with their friends. If it isn't, they share that with their friends as well—usually with a recommendation for people to boycott the brand or to spread the word so others know. There may be no better example of this than United Airlines and Dave Carroll's guitar. This story is now told in a catchy song on YouTube, in a book, and on a dedicated website, http://123.ch/uaguitar. Here's how the story is told on the website:

> "United Airlines had broken Dave's guitar in checked luggage. After eight months of pestering the company for compensation, he turned to his best tool—songwriting—and vowed to create a YouTube video about the incident that he hoped would garner a million views in one year. Four days after its launching, the first million people had watched 'United Breaks Guitars.' United stock went down 10 percent, shedding $180 million in value; Dave appeared on outlets as diverse as CNN and The

View. United relented. And throughout the business world, people began to realize that 'efficient' but inhuman customer-service policies had an unseen cost—brand destruction by frustrated, creative, and socially connected customers."

Marketing is no longer your message alone. It is your message, bolstered by your customers' message. You and your customers together create your brand. That's why it's so important to understand the new consumer, a plugged in, social creature who often has extensive social reach.

The strength of social consumers was already being recognized by businesses in 2009, when Havas Worldwide performed a study on the subject. Since that time, consumers have become even more adept at leveraging social media to share their messages. Here's what Havas Worldwide found:

"The New Consumers are **smarter, more empowered,** and **more demanding** than previous *generations of shoppers. They make full use of online tools to connect with others and score the right buys.*

1. 69% of global respondents to Havas Worldwide New Consumer study say they are smarter shoppers than they were a few years ago.

2. 63% are more demanding shoppers than they used to be.

3. 62% do lots of consumer research online—e.g., seeking out product info, reviews and ratings, price comparisons.

*They seek to **align with brand partners who share their personal values***:

- 50% say it is more important to them today to feel good about the companies with which they do business.

- 57% prefer to buy from companies that share their personal values.

- 49% prefer to do business with companies that have a reputation for a purpose beyond profits (e.g., Newman's Own, The Body Shop).

- 54% believe the most successful and profitable businesses in the future will be those that practice sustainability."

Consumers today are engaged with the world around them. They care deeply about social and economic issues, and they are particular about who they do business with. So not only must you create an engaging message that stands out from the clutter, you must also communicate authentically and transparently that you share your customers' values.

Is it possible to do this? It is if you're willing to step up your game. Only through next-level content marketing can you effectively communicate who you are and what you stand for to a social, connected world.

Taking Content to the Next Level

Next-level content has two components: magnetic content and sophisticated delivery.

Magnetic content attracts your ideal prospects while turning away tire-kickers and people who aren't a good fit for your products. Yes, this approach can limit your audience size, but those who fit the profile of your target audience will not only read your content, they'll act on it. It's the perfect scenario for today's marketers. By prequalifying your prospects, you only spend time selling to the people most likely to buy from you.

The second component, sophisticated delivery, requires more than a PDF. To take your content to the next level, you need a delivery format that engages and provides a stellar user experience while giving you the feedback you need to measure and improve your content.

Next-level content surprises and delights the end user. It also fills the feedback loop that content marketing has been missing up to this point—insight on how users respond to your content. Given that both these elements are present, you have the resources to drive traffic, engage your audience, tell your brand's story and spread your message.

Our challenge now is to take your content to the next level. That's what we talk about in this book. Fair warning: This isn't an introduction to content marketing. This book is for marketers who understand the mechanics of content marketing and are ready to take it to the next level.

We cover magnetic content, content delivery, and traffic. We also cover topics that are rarely talked about in relation to content marketing: branding and the sales moment. But all of these elements are necessary for next-level content marketing. Leave any of them out, and you won't get the results promised by content marketing advocates. Put them all together, and you'll have a content marketing machine that drives business and builds your profits.

Shall we begin?

24   Ted Box

Chapter 2

How to Create Magnetic Content

Next-level content marketing starts with your message. Just as Bill Gates predicted, today's consumers expect deep and up-to-date information that they can explore at will. They want multiple formats that are easy to access on multiple devices. They want to be able to personally respond, whether by engaging with the author or sharing with their friends and followers.

That's a big assignment. And it requires more than a skilled writer or creative team. It requires an ability to see the big picture, not just the words on the screen. You need to be able to balance the needs of your audience with the needs of your business.

Content May be King, but Context Is the Crown

The typical approach to any marketing activity is to create a workflow and automate as much as possible. For content marketers, that can be fatal. When you disengage your brain and stop thinking about what you're doing, the result is content for content's sake. Articles, brochures and eBooks are produced simply to meet deadlines and fulfill the requirements of your editorial calendar. That kind of content does not wear the crown. I call it hamster-wheel marketing, and it will never win customers or achieve your business goals.

Leading marketers understand that each time you publish, you teach people whether to engage with you or ignore you. Even one negative experience reading your content can teach people never to click through, that reading your message is a waste of their valuable time. This results in unsubscribes, not loyal readership.

Content must be relevant, otherwise it just adds to the noise. If it doesn't address a question or a challenge your customer is facing right now, and if it doesn't entertain or fulfill on its promise, it's likely to be filtered out. That's what differentiates next-level content. It solves real problems and shares in-depth information. It may even be entertaining, but it is always relevant and, therefore, can attract your ideal customers.

Think about that for a moment. By focusing on engaging your ideal prospects, you create content that's designed to get their attention and attract them into your funnel where you can build relationship and trust.

Sounds like a dating relationship, and it is. You must woo your ideal customer. Move too fast or come off as too desperate, and you will likely run them off. But if you keep it cool, offering one piece of useful information after another, you'll soon have a lasting, loyal customer, ready to spend years, not hours, with you.

The key is magnetism. You must attract your ideal customer and repel all others. You read that right. Next-level content actually repels people who don't fit your ideal customer profile. If that sounds exclusive, get over it. It's the only way to succeed online. By narrowing the field, you increase conversions. It's that simple.

7 Elements of Magnetic Content

Okay, so we've established that your content needs to be magnetic. Let's review the qualities of magnetic content.

It starts with the end user

Up in the Swiss Alps is a monastery where monks provide healing herbs to people who visit. This is an age-old recipe, known only to the monks, and they don't sell it or advertise it in any way. It's purely a ministry, with an interesting side effect: After taking the herbs, people often end up with thicker, more luxurious hair.

Interested? So was a visiting businessman, who we'll call Eric to protect the innocent. Eric was so intrigued by what he heard from others, he visited the monastery hoping to learn the monks' secret formula and be able to produce and sell the cure for baldness. Naturally, the monks weren't interested in sharing their secret formula, especially if there was a chance that it would be commercialized, so they refused to tell him how they made it. They did, however, offer him a bagful of healing herbs for his own personal use.

Thinking that the bag would give him the information he sought, Eric happily accepted. He then had the solution analyzed using Gas Chromatography–Mass Spectrometry (GC-MS) which is an analytical method that combines the features of gas-liquid chromatography and mass spectrometry to identify different substances within a sample to accurately identify the individual ingredients. There was just one problem. The GC-MS didn't seem to give him the proper ratios. So even though he identified every component in his little bag of healing herbs, years later, he was still no closer to the secret that produces the amazing side-effect.

This is exactly what happens to many marketers. They learn the ingredients of an important tactic, such as magnetic content, but they can't seem to reproduce it on their own. One reason, as I've already mentioned, is that they're hamster-wheel marketers, too busy fulfilling their content quota rather than engaging their brains and creating something valuable. But another is that they focus too closely on the list of ingredients. They aren't finding the right process or delivery mechanism to make it yield the desired results.

Because you create content, send it to a designer, then publish it, and only then get customer feedback, it's easy to think that your readers come last in the content equation. After all, you create content to build your business and keep the marketing wheels turning, so that should come first, right?

Wrong.

Content must start with the end user. Otherwise it never reaches its destination. It just languishes on your blog or in someone's email inbox because it's not interesting enough to earn a click.

Fortunately, Eric understood this. You see, he's a hairdresser and could immediately see how the monks' herbal solution could benefit his clients. Balding men would love it because it could restore their hair. Women would flock in droves to use it because of another unusual side effect: Not only does this solution cause your hair to grow in thicker, it causes it to come back in its original color.

Now that's relevant! Who doesn't want to keep a full head of hair in its natural color, with no dyes or chemicals of any kind?

It took Eric 40 years to hone in on the precise formula, but he finally did it. While his marketing isn't where it needs to be, I fully expect him to sell crate-loads of his product. Why? He understands his customers. And he's willing to go to great lengths to deliver value. What's more, all he has to do is share his story with people, and he'll have their attention. It's relevant. It's engaging. And for people who want to hide any evidence of aging, it's fascinating.

Magnetic content starts with the end user. Whatever your story or product may be, keep in mind that its value is measured by your audience, not you. Even if your product is as boring as bolts, you need to understand what makes it valuable to your audience. What's unique about it? What problem does it solve? And what lengths are you willing to go to in delivering it to your audience?

It delivers amazement

Don't let this word confuse you. When I say content should be amazing, I'm not talking about hype. Here, I'm talking about the relevance of the message, how valuable it is in your customers' eyes, and its quality across the board: in the writing, the layout, and the delivery.

When you surprise and delight your audience, you've hit the mark. For that, you may need to share a more interesting story, go deeper with your insights, share more details, or provide a format that makes it easier to understand.

Your goal is the highest possible value, the best possible deliverable. You must always ask yourself, "Is this good enough, or can I give more?"

It shares passion

Your core message must be shared with passion and energy. I have a phrase for this. I call it *eating your own dog food*. In essence, if you don't believe in your product enough to use it yourself, then you don't believe in it. If you don't follow your own advice, I have to wonder what's wrong with it.

If you're passionate about your product or message, you'll share it with the world. You'll get the word out because you honestly believe it will change the world and improve people's lives—like Eric's hair tonic. You see, Eric does indeed use his own product, and though he is in his eighties, his hair is as thick and dark at was in his twenties. The fact that he spent 40 years perfecting the formula speaks to his passion. The fact that he uses it himself proves it!

That level of passion is contagious. It shines through your words and adds vitality to your videos. It also attracts your ideal customers like bees to a field of clover. This is where magnetism starts. If you aren't passionate about your product, you may as well lock up and shut down. You won't be able to cut through the clutter, because your message will fall flat.

Sorry. That's just the way it is.

It adds value

This is an interesting one, so I want you to pay attention. We've had clients call us up and tell us they need an app that delivers value to their customers. Many of these people are on the right track. They've heard that it's important to deliver value, but they have missed the point.

Here's why: Value is not something you manufacture. Value, remember, is in the eye of the customer. It's the "extra" that makes people's lives easier. It's the little things you do to make them believe that you're unique and amazing. Remember also that this isn't anything new. Your job has always been to create value for your readers in the form of compelling content.

If you have years of experience creating content that your readers valued, whether in print or digitally, then don't worry. You're already there. If not, don't look for bells and whistles that will add value. Go out and talk to your target audience. Ask them what they care about and what problems they need to solve. Adding value can be as simple as resolving those problems.

What you think is valuable and what they think is valuable may be polar opposites. But you won't know that until you spend some quality time with the end users.

It's simple

Don't complicate your message or your solutions. Simplify your audience's life, and they will not only listen to you, they'll likely do anything you ask them to do.

The reason is clear. A complicated message can't be understood, and most people won't bother trying to decipher it. A complicated solution requires more work than the problem itself, so most people will roll their eyes and move on. People are already too busy and too stressed. They don't need you to make it worse.

While it's true that complexity tends to impress people—and they often think it sounds smart—they're actually drawn to and are most likely to respond to simplicity. Robert B. Cialdini, in his book *Yes!*, cites the power of simplicity in driving people to act. He said, "Readers mistakenly interpret the sense of difficulty they feel when they read a message with…as a sense of difficulty believing the content of the message."

High-value content is surprisingly simple. Make that your goal, and you'll likely see more engagement and higher response levels.

It's actionable

High-value content empowers people to succeed. For that, you should never stop sharing your ideas. Tell people how to do it themselves, and they'll love you for it.

Don't get selfish here. There is a misunderstanding, prevalent among marketers, that if you share the recipe to your secret sauce, people will stop buying your sauce. Nothing could be further from the truth. Telling people how you do what you do builds credibility and often increases sales.

Why? People want to simplify their lives. In most cases, they'd rather pay you to do something for them than invest time and energy into figuring it out themselves. They do, however, want to be sure they're choosing the right person to hire. If your content provides more details and more in-depth instructions of how it's done, you overcome their fears and win their trust. When they're ready to take action, you're the logical choice.

It's interactive

People hate lectures. They love conversations, especially one-on-one chats with someone they respect. Treat content like a conversation. Invite response. To do this, you need to be fully committed to social marketing. And you need to include social elements in all your content:

- a social media module so they can share pages or paragraphs of your content with their followers, friends and family

- push notifications so you can deliver breaking news related to your audience's interests (especially if you have a niche publication)

- tap-to-call services so your readers can call you or your advertisers directly from within your publication using the phone of their choice

- email integration so you can build the relationship and your list

Remember, we live in the Connected Age. Give people a way to interact, respond, to talk back, and you've got them engaged.

Creating Magnetic Content

Okay, so you know what separates magnetic content from the pack. How do you create it?

Your process is probably unique. That's okay. If you're already successfully creating content, you probably don't need instructions on how to do it. But if your end result falls short of magnetic, you may need a slight adjustment to the way you think about content.

Write to one person, your ideal customer

We're going to get exclusive again. When creating your content, imagine yourself writing to one person. If you know someone who fits the profile of your ideal customer, pretend you're writing to that one person. If not, create a persona, or imaginary person, with all the qualities of your ideal customer, and focus on him as you write directly to him in the second person (using "you" rather than "he" or "they"). Perhaps you've already noticed that I eat my own ice cream, and this book is no exception.

Sometimes that's all it takes to level up and take your content up a notch. By narrowing your focus, you actually change the quality of your writing, replacing broad generalizations with specifics and providing information that's actually useful rather than tossing around industry catch phrases and jargon.

Focus on pull, not push

Most marketers get lazy. Since their job is to promote a product, they put their energy into pushing features and benefits above everything else. After all, that's what sales is about, right? Well, maybe, but not really. By focusing on your product first, you end up with the dreaded monologue—an uptight, selfish marketer only interested in hearing his own voice. You simply can't create the dialog today's consumer wants (and needs) before they buy using that approach.

Reverse that tendency, and you'll get better results. Keep your focus on your reader's problems. Talk about your own brand only as it relates to those problems, and your content will become instantly more magnetic.

Treat every prospect as unique

It's important to consider that different "types" of people buy from you, each unique, often with their own particular set of requirements. You may need to segment your market, creating a specific message for each group you serve. (Otherwise you may slip into generalizations, and as we discussed above, you need to speak one-on-one to your audience.)

For example, you may sell to B2B customers as well as B2C customers, or you may offer different services to large and small companies. Resist the temptation to lump these different groups together. While it seems easier to create one message to address them both, a smarter practice is to create Web pages and content for each segment, so you can zero in on their needs.

Always offer more

So you finished a blog post or an eBook. So what? How can you add more value? Put yourself in your readers' shoes and try to imagine what they want from you. Would they benefit from a real-life example, a checklist, or a list of resources? If so, add it. Be generous to a fault.

Leverage data to improve messaging over time

If you ever feel overwhelmed by analytics, remember that data for data's sake is as useful as content for content's sake—not at all. The data you gather from analytics is a gold mine for your content marketing. In it are many of the secrets you need to create next-level content: Which messages resonate? What topics get the most readership and engagement? Which seem to get no traction at all? Who are the people who seem most attracted to your content, and where are they located?

Here's where you can separate leading marketers from hamster-wheel marketers. Leading marketers don't treat content as once-and-done projects. Instead, they treat them as tests. They go through the process as usual, writing and publishing content. But then they dive into the data, and use their newly found insight to refine their message and improve engagement. Lather, rinse, repeat. It's a continuous cycle of content creation and improvement that gets better results over time.

Make technology work for you

Technology changes daily. And while that may seem burdensome to a busy content creator, it's also a responsibility. Remember, your audience is experimenting with new technology, in many cases, as soon as it comes out. They play with it in their games and apps, and often create new and creative ways to use it in their personal lives.

Then they come to your content, which relies on old technology because you were too busy to figure out how new systems work. Not only does this make you immediately irrelevant, it brands you as outdated. For consumers who want new solutions and cutting-edge information, you've just communicated that you aren't their best resource.

I'm sorry to break it to you, but you have to keep up with technology. If you can take advantage of it to improve your user experience, by all means, invest the time and effort to do so. Stay current, or die. It's that important.

A great resource to help you with that is @TechCrunch or, if you want more specific information, subscribe to one of their Feedburner feeds here: http://123.ch/techcrunch. One other way I enjoy keeping alert and up-to-date is by using Google Alerts to monitor the Web for interesting new content: http://123.ch/alerts.

Guidelines for Creating Content

The structure of your content depends on your purpose. In general, you want to do one of two things: drive action or build relationship.

For content that drives action—like brochures, sales collateral, and advertorials—you need to use a direct response format. Start with your hook. Present your benefits and proof elements, and wind up with a strong call to action.

For content that generates leads and builds relationship—freemiums, eBooks, and special reports, for instance—you want to tone down the sales pitch. Your goal here is to be as generous as possible, so you can leverage the Law of Reciprocity. Give, give, give, and then finally ask for something in return. It's a process that's been scientifically proven to elicit a favorable response.

Let's look at some structures that will help you achieve these goals.

A structure that drives action

This is one of those killer frameworks that you can use to create content and collateral that drive action. Simply copy the format and insert your own message as appropriate.

Problem-Solution

- The hook
- The problem
- The implication
- The solution
- The result
- The close
- Add more value

Here's an example for the weight-loss niche:

1. The Hook: These days, you have around 9 seconds to hook people. Give them some bait (preferably in the form of a story). You've seen these sorts of pitches before; it's the classic infomercial format.

"I was 200lbs overweight and within a short 30-day period, I managed to lose 80lbs and get into the best shape of my life, looking good, feeling great & fit for the beach. All without any exercises. What I discovered was a simple food hack that I'm going to share with you in a moment."

2. The Problem: What were the key frustrations you had when you were trying to achieve your goal?

"When I first started out, I had no motivation. I was just so overweight. I did not feel like going to the gym. I did not know what to eat..."

3. The Implication: What will happen if you don't fix this?

"If you continue down this path, you risk losing your friends, gaining more weight and watching your health deteriorate."

4. The Solution: What I did...

"I went online and found this amazing program called XYZ weight loss and I tried it."

5. The Result: To my amazement...

"I lost 80lbs in 30 days."

6. The Close: I had an amazing result, my life has changed...

"Would you like to achieve results like this in your own life? If you do, let me tell you about my brand new product XYZ... here's what you need to do next."

Add the key benefits for this product. Then review each of the benefits and wrap up with a call to action.

CTA:

"So, if you want to fix these problems today and get away from the frustrations that you are currently experiencing, change your life right now, go ahead and click the buy button below to get started."

Need another, more in-depth structure? Here you go.

1. Introduction that Focuses the Viewer

   - Create a Connection with the viewer
   - Establish a connection between the viewer and the problem or situation.
   - Confirm Credibility
   - Confirm Ownership of the Solution.
   - Create Frame of Reference

2. Identify with the Problem or situation

   - Align ourselves with the understanding of the problem
   - Present Us v Them Argument

- Create Credibility by deconstructing existing narratives

3. **Highlight the Problem's Negatives**

   - Discuss the Problem's Negatives
   - Highlight the effects of inaction
   - Set up our solution as THE SOLUTION

4. **Deliver a Powerful Solution**

   - Present our solution's Name
   - Reason(s) for superiority

5. **Highlight the Benefits of the Solution**

   - Address Each Issue and Driving Emotion of the Problem
   - Connect Each Issue and Driving Emotion to the Product's Benefits
   - Summarize the Product or Services Benefits

6. **Provide Social Proof**

    - Include Quotes from Customers
    - Present Reviews or Testimonials
    - Show Customer's Experiencing Benefits

7. **Create Desire**

    - Highlight Special Offers
    - Scarcity
    - Bandwagon

8. **Set up the Call to Action**

    - Illustrate Life after Solution

9. **Logical Reasoning for Action**

    - Give viewer several logical reasons to act.
    - Tell them the reason they would tell their partner they acted.
    - Use Assumptive Close to Process

10. Highlight the Continuation of the Problem

- Remind Viewer that Problem will continue with inaction
- Appeal to Emotion, Reason, and Logic one final time.
- List possible Negatives

A structure that builds relationship

With today's time-strapped consumer, even if you want to drive action, you must first engage and delight. In other words, you need to put more focus into relationship than into driving action. For that, you need to decide how you're offering value and use the structure that seems most appropriate. Here are two options.

Promise-Proof

This is a useful structure for thought leadership pieces. It's perfect for educating and inspiring readers.

- Create a picture that hooks people's interest.
- Make a deep promise that your audience already wants.
- Prove it works.
- Tell them what to do next. (CTA should be for engagement, not sales.)

Here's an example from a blog post by Kathryn Aragon: http://123.ch/promiseproof.

The article begins by tapping into people's assumption that the best way to network is at a conference or event, then promises that they can achieve the same thing through Twitter. It recounts an actual network-building exchange, then gives tips for readers to get similar results.

Problem-Solution

Problem-Solution formats aren't only for direct response. They can also build relationship, by offering helpful information that solves your reader's problems, thereby positioning you as an authority.

- Introduce the problem.
- Introduce your solution.
- Explain the steps or details as specifically as possible.
- Add more value.

Here's an example from a KinetiZine, The Cure for the Common Brochure: http://123.ch/problemsolution

This is a longer piece of content addressing a problem we all face as marketers, creating engaging content. The solution is to include more kinetic, or dynamic elements. These are explained in detail beginning on page nine. Then, in the final pages of the brochure, we add value by giving readers evaluative questions and resources to improve their own brochures.

Creating magnetic content requires more than a hamster-wheel mentality. You can't automate too much. You can't assume you know your audience. And you can't be lazy. Magnetic content attracts readers and rewards their attention. But true engagement requires more than interesting topics and excellent writing. In Chapter 3, we talk about content delivery, the often-ignored side of content marketing.

Chapter 3

Improving Content Delivery

If you're a content marketer, you probably agree, content creation seems to take most of our time. We're constantly focused on creating the right story for our brand. We focus on refining our voice and creating a more conversational, more accessible style. We worry about the design, laboring over an eye-catching layout and images that could be hung in the Louvre.

But having a smart message and beautiful layout aren't enough. For next-level content marketing, you also need to think about what happens *after* you've created the perfect piece of content. You need to think about your delivery format, measurement, and cycles of optimization so you get the best possible results from your content.

To do that, it's important to understand the environment that your content faces once released to the world. Let's take a moment to review the challenges you face, namely, attention deficit and an inability to track results.

Your biggest enemy: attention deficit

The biggest enemy of content marketers is attention deficit. I don't care who they are, your audience is time-starved and distracted. This condition isn't restricted to any one segment of society; it's pandemic. In fact, it's been suggested that, based on the scarcity of time, we now live in an attention economy.

It's a relatively simple concept. This explanation comes from Elisa Gabbert, in her article on WordStream:

"The idea is that we're all competing for a finite amount of attention, and it's a zero-sum game. If people are paying attention to your competitor, they can't pay attention to you at the same time.

Another term for the same basic idea is 'attention economics' – in an attention economy, attention is treated as a scarce commodity. We've got access to more information than ever before, but no more time or attention to give."

It makes sense. As more information is shoved in front of us, we have to pick and choose what we pay attention to. But there's more to the concept than that. At its root, "attention economy" has more to do with economics than you might originally think. Let's look at a quote from Michael H. Goldhaber in a 1997 Wired article:

"As the Net becomes an increasingly strong presence in the overall economy, the flow of

> *attention will not only anticipate the flow of money, but eventually replace it altogether."*

Money follows attention? It's a radical idea, but worth exploring, especially for content marketers. If it's true, your profitability is directly connected to your ability to get people's attention and hold it. This makes your ability to create attention-grabbing content much more than a popularity contest. It ties your content's success or failure to your business success.

Let's assume for a moment that the issue is indeed that critical. What are you dealing with? You must create content for people who don't have time to read it. Yet you must be able to get their attention, transform them into readers, and, ultimately, into loyal customers—with your content.

The challenge is that even people who would classify themselves as readers don't have time to read. At best, they're skimmers, who scan to get the gist of an article before deciding whether it's worth their time to read.

This is your audience. You only have a few seconds to wow them enough to get them engaged. That's not new information, I realize. But it is key. It's why you've probably been instructed to spend an inordinate amount of time on your headline. And though that's a good place to start, your effort shouldn't stop there.

Your audience judges your content by its appearance even more than the headline. In a split second, they take in your layout, color choices, and general appearance. The quality of this first impression determines whether or not you get those few second to wow them with your headline and lead.

In the first split second your visitors view your website—before they ask what it's about or whether it's for them—they make a quick assessment: Is this up-to-date? Is it high-quality? How professional is it? The answers they arrive at determine whether you get their attention for a few more seconds so you can answer their question, "What's in it for me?"

That being the case, you need to make sure your first impression is good. These six things are what matter most when you are trying to reach distracted readers, who I often think of as "attention sparrows."

Get creative with your layout

When it comes to layout, my personal favorite is Apple. Their clean, uncluttered layout style is perfect for their audience: creative, colorful people who care about quality as much as functionality. Take a quick break to review Apple's home page, or any page on their website for that matter. Even at first glance, it communicates class and quality. After viewing their page, does it even cross your mind to question the quality of their products? For the average consumer, no.

Keep in mind, I'm not suggesting that all layouts should imitate Apple. Apple stands out because they identified their target audience and created a look and feel that resonates (and even attracts) them. Their look and feel might not work for a financial institution, a pet store, or a supplier of survival gear. You need to design a layout that works for *your* brand and *your* audience.

Creativity is the key. By that, I mean that you should come up with a look and feel that's all your own. Creativity isn't faddish. It doesn't copy what everyone else is doing. It is strategic and smart. For instance, Mashable began using Parallax technology to showcase its feature articles in early 2014. It was ground-breaking for a blog to look so much like a magazine, and it immediately set a new standard for online content. It also set Mashable apart. Now, every time I see a feature article presented in Parallax, I think of Mashable. Since I saw them do it first, I think of them as the leader in this trend.

When it comes to your content, you should never sacrifice readability, clarity, and communication. But you should try to add engaging elements that keep people from getting bored. Advanced content marketers today don't settle for ordinary. Not all posts are written articles with one image. Some include video or audio. Others may have interactive elements, such as animations or Vine videos. This creates more variety and sets this marketer's site apart from mediocre sites. And this probably earns them a few more seconds to hook their readers' attention.

What about your brochures and eBooks. Many content marketers, even today, publish these in print form. Others simply take their print layout and publish it as a PDF. Is that really the most impressive use of technology today? With technology making the strides it has in recent years, same-old same-old publishing simply isn't enough. Your overall presentation must stand out—like Mashable's Parallax articles and the digital billboard we talked about at the beginning of this book. You must set yourself apart from the crowd, so you can earn a few more seconds of eye contact.

Differentiate yourself

We've talked about the need to stand out from the pack, do something different, and do something that's uniquely you. As you strive to do this, beware of two mistakes I often see. One is to overstate your differences; the other is to understate them.

Some people think they can differentiate themselves by leveraging an element of shock in their marketing. They add curse words to their marketing, display outrageous attitudes, or make unbelievable claims. But unless that's the real you and you've created a brand that appeals to people who like those tactics, it's not creative. It's just overblown.

There's a place for authenticity. It's possible that your personality is honestly outrageous. But if you're trying to make a statement with your style rather than just being yourself, you're probably copycatting someone you've seen and admired. Sorry, that's no way to differentiate.

The other mistake marketers make is to be so reserved, they blend into the crowd. Basically, they take no risks, holding onto "the way it's always been" as long as possible and thinking that they're just playing it safe. In fact, the opposite is true. These marketers often appear to be very busy, but their effort yields little fruit.

In my job, I get to meet thousands of marketers and most seem to have been infected by this virus. Honestly, it's the best analogy I can come up with. I see busy people who barely have time to sit down for a meal, constantly tweeting and tooling and putting in hours that even Edison would consider insane. I've given this virus a name. It's the hamster-wheel virus, and, as you probably guess, it infects hamster-wheel marketers.

These people are easy to spot. They are the busiest people you'll ever meet, but they don't seem to make any progress. They're doing what they've always done, using what they've always used, and not moving projects forward. Then they take a break, change jobs, firms, organizations, etc., and start the gestation cycle all over again.

The virus seems to target marketers, but they aren't alone. As it turns out, this is a virus that crosses all job descriptions. The infected find it challenging to keep up with peers and get easily overwhelmed with the vast choices technology offers today. They are often not able to make a decision. So, although we have more tools available for marketers today than ever before and although some of these tools are truly incredible, these marketers don't take action. It seems that analysis paralysis sets in and takes hold, and they become convinced that it's safer not to stand out.

These people are so risk-averse, they can't succeed as marketers. That's not a judgment; it's a fact. Marketing depends on your ability to differentiate yourself. You *must* stand out. But hamster-wheel marketers are afraid to make a statement that goes against the grain.

Nothing saddens me more than hamster-wheel marketers. There was a time when marketing was the bastion of creativity in the organization. But that level of creativity is rare today. Imagine if more marketers were to get infected. We'd run out of creative energy altogether!

Here's what to watch out for. Symptoms include a strong, overwhelming desire to play it safe and an omnipresent fear of rocking the boat and changing the status quo. You can usually identify it through copycat marketing. The infected don't think for themselves, not even to evaluate their work and figure out what makes them unique.

Inoculate yourself. You *must* take time to differentiate. We cover it in depth in Chapter 6 of this book. But for now, be aware, powerful brands aren't different for the sake of being different. But neither are they afraid to be different. Apple is the perfect example of this. Take a moment to listen to Steve Jobs introducing the iPhone in 2007 (http://123.ch/jobs). Pay attention to the litany of breakthrough products Apple created, beginning with the home computer. Apple is the powerhouse of technology because it leads rather than following. It is unafraid of being different. It doesn't have an appearance of busy-ness; rather, it is busy creating technology that most other people only dream about. Differentiation creates a powerful brand. And it earns the loyalty of appreciative customers.

Here's what I want you to remember. Just as Apple distinguishes itself by creating innovative products people love, your differentness should create value for your audience. If your customers need a maverick leader and if you do, in fact, have a maverick personality, then leverage it. It's honest and relevant. But if your audience is a relatively clean-cut sort of a group, and you try to "be yourself" by cussing at them, you're more likely to scare them off.

Be real. Be different. But more important, be the best version of yourself that can meet your customers' deepest needs.

Think outside the box

What will get eyeballs on your content? That's what matters most. What makes it easy for people to focus on your message? That's your second consideration.

When it comes to content marketing, these are your two most important tasks: getting people to pay attention for a few seconds more, and then making your ideas so easy to absorb that even scanners will get them. For that, you can't be lazy. You can't just do what everyone else is doing. You must think outside the box and do something unique.

We've talked a little about the unique things other content marketers are doing. But are you limited by that? Of course not! You should always be watching for new ways to showcase your message so it communicates better, is more relevant, and offers a better user experience.

In my opinion, this is so critical to content marketing success, I've actually put money where my mouth is by creating a completely new format for delivering content. It leverages the technology available on the Web—HTML and CSS—to distribute brochures and other content that are as advanced as your Web pages. So you can create a more fluid user experience from your website to your content and back again. I mention this not to show off or even make a sale (though, if it sounds interesting, go to http://123.ch/kinetizine and check it out.) I mention this to tell you how important it is to create unique user experience.

It is critical that you think outside the box when it comes to delivering value to your customers. This is what separates the hamster-wheel marketers from leading marketers. Leading marketers don't complain or make excuses about other priorities. They don't perceive an extra task or new technology as extra work. They understand that offering value is the least they should be doing if marketing is their gig.

You Must Measure Results

We've talked about the challenge you face in an attention economy. But there's another challenge you probably fight every day, and that's the justification of your work internally—to your boss and, more important, to his boss. The need for measurable results is palpable, and the C-Suite demands evidence that your job is indeed the smart investment you say it is. The trouble is, content is particularly difficult to measure.

Oh sure, you can measure the number of downloads or page views. But that doesn't give you real insight. It only tells you the title was interesting enough to make people click through or opt in. Pit that against the website analytics your onsite content generates: page views, time on each page, the path users follow, and the bounce rate—and that's only a few of the metrics available.

What if the pages of your content—brochures, newsletters, brand magazines, etc.—were as measurable as your Web pages? You might discover that the video on page 3 gets more time than the graphic on page 5. Or that tables win big and photos don't. You could essentially test your messaging inside your content. Does chapter 2 or chapter 3 get more clicks from the Table of Contents, and how much time do readers spend on each? The one with the best clickthrough or time-on-page is obviously more important to your audience.

This kind of data can tell you who your best prospects are and what interests them most. But unless your content is equipped to give you that level of insight, you have no idea what they want to hear from you.

What to measure

Measuring results is a hot topic today, but most marketers aren't sure about what to measure. Metrics are roughly divided into two categories:

- Content metrics
- Audience metrics

Content metrics include conversion funnels, time on page, bounce rate and the number of times a hotspot is activated. These are important because they help you evaluate how your audience is interacting with your content and where they are in your sales funnel.

They help you answer questions like:

- *"What content in my brochure is the most popular?"*

- *"Are my readers getting through my sales funnel the way they should or are they getting stuck somewhere and exiting?"*

- *"How much time did my readers spend on each piece of content?"*

Audience metrics include demographics, such as age, gender, user location, mobile device and software usage.

This is important because it gives you the insight you need to increase reader retention and provide more opportunities for a sales moment.

That's why understanding metrics alone can boost your content's ROI immensely. Marketing has evolved from pushing broadcast messages and figuratively screaming from rooftops to a virtual, two-way conversation between brands and customers. Today, any message can be shared via social platforms and seen by thousands or, if it goes viral, millions. Your future sales depend on gaining and maximizing user insight. Each time a prospect engages with your digital content, you have an opportunity to listen and gain valuable information to influence the dialog and desired result.

And that, my friend, is how you justify your job to the higher ups. The numbers speak for themselves.

PDFs Are Not Your Friend

I don't have anything against PDFs. I use them all the time. But never for publishing our content because I've learned that PDFs can't provide the sophisticated experience our audience is looking for. The best case scenario is that your PDF gets read by a prospect and the content resonates. But now you've got a conversion problem in your buyer journey process. There is no way to track user engagement with the content while they are reading it, or what they do with it after they are done. Where does the user go at the end of the PDF? What is the path they follow to be converted into a qualified lead?

Blasting out PDFs limits the effectiveness of your content marketing because you won't be provided with any data on the backend. There is no content tracking platform for PDFs that will tell you if the PDF was shared, or how many new prospects discovered that PDF as a result of the original prospect's share. Without user engagement data, you are missing a critical element for driving conversions.

PDFs may have been good for broadcasting a few years ago, but today we want to know more than how many PDFs were downloaded. If PDFs don't allow us to gain insight into our prospects' behavior, why do so many marketers still use them?

I believe that there are three reasons:

1. Most marketers are not aware that PDFs are holding them back like a ball and chain. Because their competitors are still using PDFs, they haven't considered that new technology could take their content to the next level.

2. Many marketers are focused on half the content equation. They enjoy producing content and don't want to bother with "what comes next." As a

result, they aren't interested in improved delivery or measurement.

3. Many marketers have the hamster-wheel virus and are afraid to evaluate the effectiveness of their methods. They are so busy doing what they've always done, they can't imagine adopting new processes, because that might incur more work.

Look for a Content Delivery Format That...

Removes technological barriers to creativity

As stated above, PDFs are not the solution to the engagement equation. PDFs were the first attempt at digitizing books and brochures, much like the Guttenberg press was the first attempt to mechanize print. Early technology is usually good for a time, but it generally gets improved upon and goes out of date pretty quickly. We've reached that point with content.

Don't stop at PDFs. Look for content delivery platforms that allow you to take full advantage of technology, adding all the features and functionality available on websites.

Allows you to add elements that actually engage

Creating interactive content that is optimized for engagement seems easy enough in theory. However, savvy marketers know that interactive content must be tailored and personalized to meet the needs of and capture the attention of their prospects.

What is engaging? That depends on your audience. But in general, movement, variety, and uniqueness capture people's attention. Look for a content platform that allows you to embed animations, video, and audio, as well as links and pop-ups.

Gives you metrics on the behavior that matters

The only way to transform your ideas into something that resonates with your audience is to adopt an optimization mindset. You need to get feedback from your audience and then make changes based on that feedback.

Start by identifying your ideal audience. Who engages with your content? Who responds to your message? Analytics give you this feedback, so you can continually improve your message and target your market.

Most content delivery platforms don't give you the feedback you need to make these decisions. If at all possible, keep pushing until you find one that does.

Allows you to include response mechanisms inside your content

Measuring user behavior allows you to identify hot prospects. But having identified them, why wouldn't you immediately respond to them? Your ideal content delivery platform should allow you to use lead-nurturing technology inside the pages of your content, just as you do on your website.

For instance, what if you're planning a webinar related to the information you share on page 5? You can set up a rule that segments users who spend more than 3 minutes on page 5. Then, a few days before the webinar, send this list a special discount.

Technically, this means your content platform needs rulesets as well as analytics, so you can set up automated responses to target behavior. If this seems confusing, it's probably because you aren't used to seeing it in content. But think about the functionality available on your website. In a blog post about email marketing, you can include an ad for a product that teaches a new email marketing strategy. When people click, they're taken to a landing page that promotes the product. If they are interested, people enter their email and download the product. In the meantime, their email is added to your list and they are automatically dripped an email series teaching advanced strategies, leading up to a backend offer for a higher cost product.

This is how we move people through a conversion funnel online. Why should it come to a screeching halt once they download your high-value content? Why shouldn't you be able to do something similar in your free report?

Here are two examples of how you might do that.

1. You might place an ad in Facebook for the report. You ask people to opt in before downloading the report, so you have their email. In the report, you create a rule for users who spend two minutes

reviewing a flowchart on page three. These people have shown by their behavior that they are interested in more information, so in the pop-up, you offer a series of emails that explains the flowchart in detail. They opt in, and you have them automatically added to a list that drips additional information about that topic. You also build relationship and offer incentive to talk to a sales representative.

2. You might advertise a free download with no opt in. You provide three little-known solutions to a common problem and talk in-depth about two of them. Then, on page eight, you place an opt-in gate. In order to see the last solution, which is the most effective of the three, readers must opt in. Rather than asking readers to opt in *before* delivering value, you are able to demonstrate how clear and useful your report is. At this point, readers are more than happy to share their email for the last and final tip. And now you have a list,

not of tire kickers, but of qualified prospects who like your approach to the problem. You also have the insight needed to begin building a profile for each prospect, so you can deliver on the promise of one-to-one marketing.

Your content delivery platform needs to be able to identify and segment your prospects based on their behavior. At the very least, you should be able to discover prospects curious enough to read about your new product line and queue them up for a special offer on autopilot.

As you can see, creative, useful content isn't the only concern for next-level content marketing. You need an advanced delivery format that allows you to gather insight and set rules for automated workflows. Now let's dive into optimization of your content. What do you do with the behavior insight you gather from your readers? Keep reading to find out.

Chapter 4

Repeating and Improving the Cycle

If you're committed to improving your content, doing whatever it takes to refine your message and learn how to effectively integrate content into your sales funnel, then these last few chapters are for you. Critical to your success is the concept of optimizing your content. To do that, you must move beyond the typical content marketing conversations. You must adopt new ways of thinking about content creation and delivery.

You already have the basics. You know how to create magnetic content, and you understand the need for advanced technology integrated into your content delivery. Now let's look at some strategic tactics that will take your content to the next level.

Become a Numbers Person

If you want to improve your content and marketing results, you have to develop a love for numbers. I've worked with content creators who smugly announced, "We're writers. We're not numbers people." Frankly, if they aren't interested in numbers, they're never going to be great content creators, because they've essentially shut off their best source of feedback—analytics.

Today, when we talk about measurement, it is no longer a term used exclusively for ROI. Technology continually brings new insights into what can be measured and how you can apply that data to get better results. Monitoring user behavior identifies and exposes prospects interests and pain points, and this insight is essential for creating one-to-one marketing opportunities.

What do you need to measure? In particular, you need to look for metrics that help you identify your ideal prospects, the topics or messages that are most important to them, and how best to deliver that message.

To identify your prospects, you need to focus on demographics: geo-location, gender, age, income, hobbies, political bent, and anything else that will help you talk to them persuasively.

To identify the topics/messages your prospects are most interested in, you need to look at the pages they spend the most time on, the titles that earn clickthrough, and the pages or titles that get the most social shares. If you have a table of contents, does one heading get more clicks than any other? That may indicate a topic that your audience is particularly interested in.

To identify the best delivery methods, look at information about users' browsers and devices. This alone will tell you whether your content needs to be optimized for phone-sized or full-sized screens. Combine this information with bounce rate, and you may learn what *not* to do. If readers click through and immediately bounce, you've probably identified a usability problem that needs immediate attention.

Now, how do you do this in practice? Keep in mind, when optimizing your content, you don't need to review all the available data. That can quickly become overwhelming.

Start by asking yourself questions about how your content is performing. For instance, do my readers prefer reading on a phone or a computer, or do they prefer content in written, audio or visual format? The metrics that matter most depend upon your question. Consider which numbers will help you find the answer to your question, and focus on those numbers. Then devise a possible solution for improving your numbers.

Optimizing your message and your content isn't achieved overnight. It isn't achieved by reviewing your content against your own preferences. And it will never reach a point of perfection. With that in mind, create your best possible message in the best possible design and delivery platform. Then see how your audience responds.

Based on those numbers, tweak your content to get better results. Over time, you'll learn which layout works best and what wording seems to get the best response. You'll know the best length and the titles that resonate. But you must review the numbers to get to that point. So commit now, if you aren't already, to become a numbers person. Your future depends on it.

Listen and Respond

Sadly, most marketers aren't paying attention to people's real-time response to their offers. Yet even mid-launch, you can tweak your offer and change your strategy to improve your results—if you're watching response rates.

Interestingly, I saw this in action in a recent launch by marketing guru Dan Kennedy. He and his team at Glazer-Kennedy Insider's Circle (GKIC) were following a proven formula for a new product launch. It included three webinars that delivered high-value content, followed by a sales video presentation, which promised even more depth and breadth within the new product.

However, proven formula or not, the numbers indicated that something was amiss. While they maintained good viewer numbers on the first three webinars, as soon as the pitch began in webinar 4, viewership went into steep decline.

As numbers started coming in—disappointing all expectations, according to Dave Dee, who was the presenter for the webinars—the team quickly assessed what the problem could be and began revising their launch plan to improve results.

This is a case study in listening and responding. I don't have the final numbers, and I haven't heard whether they were satisfied with the launch results, but I was impressed with their quick assessment and response.

This is what marketing is all about. To become a next-level content marketer, you must learn to trust the numbers. They give you the insight you need to know what is working and what is not.

Talk your Customer's Language

Effective communication aligns the message with the audience's needs. So you need to understand not just the message your audience prefers, but also the style and format of that message.

In order to know their preferences, you need to know your audience. And you need to be listening to them continually. Often, they'll communicate through words, telling you through comments, emails, or one-on-one conversations what their preferences are. Other times, it's not so clear. You must read their behavior to understand their preferences.

You must give them input they understand

Remember the PC v. Mac commercials, with each computer represented by a different style of person? Mac was laid back and casual. PC was uptight and concerned with details. Essentially, each was an avatar for the two types of people who buy computers.

Now imagine selling your product to each of these personalities. To one, you might tell jokes and stories from your personal life. To the other, you'd keep it business-like and proper. If you told an off-color joke to PC, he'd probably leave the room.

Your customers may not fit perfectly into the PC or Mac personalities, but they probably can be classified in some particular way, say, as creatives, entrepreneurs, engineers, or stay-at-home moms. Messages written for creatives won't be as persuasive to engineers, and *vice versa*. Each has a different way of talking and a different way of processing information. You must create a message that's perfectly targeted to your audience.

It's like programming for your message

Our brain processes information much the way a computer does. It takes fantastic amounts of data and organizes them into a configuration that makes sense to that person. A computer can't do anything without software, which provides the structure to perform specific tasks. Meta-programs operate much the same way in our brain. They provide the structure that governs what we pay attention to, how we make sense of our experiences, and the directions in which they can take us. They provide the basis on which we decide that something is interesting or dull, a potential blessing or a potential threat.

To communicate with a computer, you have to understand its software. To communicate effectively with a person, you have to understand his meta-programs.

People have patterns of behavior, and they have patterns by which they organize their experiences to create those behaviors. Only through understanding those mental patterns can you expect to get your message across.

The most basic meta-program involves moving toward something or moving away. All human behavior revolves around the urge to gain pleasure or avoid pain. You pull away from a lighted match in order to avoid the pain of burning your hand. You sit and watch a beautiful sunset because you get pleasure from the glorious celestial show as day glides into night.

The same is true of more ambiguous actions. One person may walk a mile to work because he enjoys the exercise. Another may walk because he has a terrible phobia about being in a car. One person may read Faulkner, Hemingway, or Fitzgerald because he enjoys their prose and insight. Another might read the same writers because he doesn't want people to think of him as uneducated. He's not so much seeking pleasure as avoiding pain; he's moving away from something, not toward it.

This process is not one of absolutes. Everyone moves toward some things and away from others. No one responds the same way to each and every stimulus, although everyone has a dominant mode, a strong tendency toward one program or another. Some people tend to be enthusiastic, curious, risk takers. They may feel most comfortable moving toward something that excites them. Others tend to be cautious, wary, and protective; they see the world as a more perilous place. They tend to take actions away from harmful or threatening things rather than towards exciting ones.

To find out which way people move, ask them what they want in a relationship—a house, car, job, or anything else. Do they tell you what they want or what they don't want?

The right way to talk

If you're a businessman selling a product, you can promote it in two ways, by what it does or by what it doesn't do. You can try to sell cars by stressing that they are fast, sleek, or sexy, or you can emphasize that they don't use much gas, don't cost much to maintain, and are particularly safe in crashes. The strategy you use should depend entirely upon the preferences of your best prospects. Use the wrong meta-programs with a person, and you might as well have stayed home. You're trying to move him towards something, and all he wants is to find a good reason to back away.

Remember, a car can travel along the same path in forward or reverse. It just depends on what direction it's facing. The same is true on a personal basis. Let's say you want your child to spend more time on his schoolwork. You might tell him, "You'd better study or you won't get into a good college." Or, "Look at Henry. He didn't study, so he flunked out of school, and he's going to spend the rest of his life pumping gas. Is that they kind of life you want for yourself?" How well will that strategy work? It depends on your child. If he's primarily motivated by moving away, it might work well.

But what if he moves towards things? What if he's motivated by things that excite him, by moving towards things he finds appealing? If that's how he responds, you're not going to change his behavior by offering the example of something to move away from. You can nag until you're blue in the face, but you're talking in the wrong key. You're talking French, but the kid only understands Greek. You're wasting your time, and his. In fact, people who move toward are often angered or even resentful of those who present things to be moved away from. You could motivate your child better by saying, "If you do x, you could probably choose any school you want."

Make Usability a Priority

We're accustomed to thinking about usability when it comes to a website. But content? Is usability an issue in blog posts, newsletters, and brochures as well? The short answer is *yes,* if you want people to read your content.

It comes back to the issue of time. People don't have time to wait on a piece of content to open and format itself. They don't have time to figure out a weird layout, once it is open. They have seconds to scan your content, maybe read a few paragraphs or sections, and then they need to move on. That being the case, you must make your content as easy to use as possible. Steve Krug's mandate for websites is equally applicable to content: Don't make me think!

Write in a way that's easy on the brain

Readability is the issue here. For that, you need to create shorter paragraphs, so readers aren't put off by great blocks of text. Each paragraph break creates white space that's easy on the eye and makes your content look less imposing.

Inside your paragraphs, keep your sentences short and easy to read. Long, unwieldy sentences may have worked for Faulkner, but they aren't advisable for content writers. Each additional phrase adds complexity to your sentence, making it harder to understand quickly. It is okay to vary sentence length, but err on the side of short and simple.

Your goal? An eighth-grade reading level. Even smart people prefer it. After a day of burning brain cells to do their job, they appreciate content that's easy to read and absorb.

Keep your format intuitive

While I do encourage outside-the-box thinking and creativity, I don't want you to stray too far from the norm when formatting your content. People don't want to have to figure out your platform. It should open with a click. Pages should scroll or turn, just as your readers expect.

If your delivery platform flips pages, is the movement smooth? Does it add to the experience, or is it a distraction?

Your content should provide an enjoyable reading experience, or it will drive users away. So it's imperative that you select your delivery platform with care.

Look at Your Funnel from the Prospect's Perspective

The 3E test

Great content is enlightening, educational, and entertaining. In truth, few articles do all three. Often they're educational, but dry as toast and boring. Other times, they're enlightening or entertaining, but miss the educational side of things.

How do you hit all three? You need to write content for people. Real people. Then write as if you're talking to them. It's not hard—unless you have a hidden agenda, such as ranking for search engines, selling, or impressing people with your advanced writing skills (give me a break!).

To enlighten people, share something they haven't heard before. Maybe you've had a brainstorm or you improved a key process. Your insights will enlighten your readers, if you're willing to share.

To educate, always add some practical tips to apply the insight you just shared.

To entertain, just be real. Don't try to impress. Talk as if you're talking to your best friend, and you'll probably nail it.

Give real answers, not just teasers

Some content marketers are afraid to share everything they know. They're afraid people will use their ideas and not need their services or products. To avoid that happening, they always try to hold something back.

As a result, their content is flimsy, at best. It never gives the whole answer to a question or the full solution to a problem. It's a teaser, not a true piece of content. If you want to frustrate your readers to death, and if you want them to unsubscribe as quickly as they can find the link, go ahead with this strategy.

But if you want loyal readers who see your brand as a go-to resource, then turn your thinking around. You are in business to serve people; they reward your generosity with their business. So be generous. Share your knowledge freely. That's the point of content, after all.

Create opportunities to respond

As you share your ideas, you're going to create *aha!* moments. You don't have to try to do this. It just happens when you're doing content marketing well. Ideally, you will provide a way for people to respond at the exact moment of the *aha!* Perhaps it's a pop-up with a call to action, a click-to-call button, or a share button so they can share your content with their followers.

This is why you want a content delivery platform that has the full functionality of the social Web. Your content platform should never stop people from responding at the moment they are ready to do so. Otherwise, they'll forget, or the excitement will fade, and they're no deeper into your funnel than they were before they opened your content.

For content to support your funnel, it needs to have the full functionality of a website—whether it sits on your site, in an app, or is a stand-alone piece of content.

Don't Manhandle Your Prospects

Bottom line, you never want to disrespect your audience. You can do that by talking down to them or being rude, but you can also do that by manhandling them, forcing them to move through your funnel at *your* pace and through the doorways *you* think are important.

Remember, people's thinking is like a computer's programming, which means some people are PCs and some are Macs. Each comes to your website with different questions and different needs. Your job is to anticipate that and provide different doorways for them to enter your funnel, depending upon their motivations and desires.

Don't force them to start with content A, then move to content B, and then, finally, to content C. Maybe they've been researching the topic for months now and are ready for content C at their first visit. Maybe they don't care about the discussion in A or C and want to read content B first. Be sensitive to your visitors' needs. Provide multiple doors for them to get in, and allow them to move around the funnel on their own path, no matter how weird it may look to you.

As a content creator, you need to anticipate the information people need, the questions they're asking, and the objections they'll likely raise. Every piece of content you create needs to address one of these topics. Address it fully and provide all the answers you can. Never withhold information believing that you can force people to move from one piece of content to another on a specific path you create. Never raise a question in one piece and answer it in another. Each piece of content should stand alone, delving deep into the topic and answering all questions related to it.

Think Two-Way, Not One-Way Delivery

The point is to keep people inside your funnel. You want them to keep downloading your content and to read each new piece you create. For that to happen, you have to make it engaging and authentic.

Keep it social and interactive

Conversational writing can make a difference. People want to be able to engage with your brand. They also want to be able to share it with their friends—assuming, of course, that it's worth sharing.

Always add share buttons. Always provide a way for readers to contact you: an email or phone number. If you can also add hot spots, pop-ups, and other interactive functionality, by all means, do so.

Keep it real

Most corporate content is mind-numbingly boring yet many manage to get thousands of followers thanks to simple brand recognition or offering bribes for likes. Old Spice and Taco Bell are different. They've each built big social media fan bases by being funny and real. This is something all those boring brands need to learn. It's not about marketing. It's about being authentic.

Take a look at the Twitter exchange on the next page. It feels a little like you're hanging out with them at the local bar.

Consumers are looking for brands they can trust. By being authentic and accessible, you open the doors for them to engage with you as if you're a real person. And since people buy from people, that's a good place to be.

TACO BELL @TacoBell 9 Jul
@OldSpice Is your deodorant made with really old spices?
Details

Old Spice
@OldSpice

 Following

@TacoBell Depends. Do you consider volcanos, tanks and freedom to be spices?

← Reply ↻ Retweet ★ Favorite

122 RETWEETS **69** FAVORITES

2:12 PM - 9 Jul 12 via web · Embed this Tweet

Reply to @OldSpice @TacoBell

Rocketfish Products @RocketfishReady 11 Jul
@OldSpice @TacoBell Before you guys get us all in trouble, we want to clarify that our products contain neither rockets nor fish.

People enjoy engaging with brands that talk like people, not businesses.

Over on the customer service side, the same holds true. Here's how Amazon delivered on their promise in 2014. You can see the original here:

http://123.ch/amazonchat.

Here's a transcript of the chat conversation (with typos and misspellings included):

You are now connected to Amazon from Amazon.com

Me: Tracking shows delivered by shipment not recieved

Amazon: Warmest greeting [name], my name is Thor.

Me: Greeting, Thor. Can I be Odin?

Amazon: Odin, Father, How art thy doing on this here fine day?

Me: Thor, my son, Agony raises upon my life.

Amazon: This is outrageous! Who dares defy The All Father Odin! What has occurred to cause this agony?

Me: I am afraid the book I ordered to defeat our enemies has been misplaced. How can we keep Valhalla intact without our sacred book.

Amazon: This is blasphemy! Wherever this book has been taken to, I shall make it my duty to get it back to you! I fear it is Loki but I dare not blame him for such things. I shall have your fortune retuned to you and thereafter we can begin to create a new quest in order to get the book back to you.

Me: Very well my son.

Amazon: Allow me some time to round up my allies and complete this please Father.

Me: Do it for me Thor, but most importantly do it for the mortals whose destiny (and grades) rely on this book.

Amazon: Alas, the treasure has been returned to you. You now need to reinstate the book into your archive so that you may yet receive it soon. I shall have the Valkyrie deliver it to you as fast as their wings can move.

Me: Ok so roleplay aside I have my money back and I reorder the book?

Amazon: haha yes I have refunded you and you need to reorder the book.

Me: Great!

Amazon: Have you placed that order?

Me: let me do that. Done

Amazon: okay let me edit it for you. [blank] That good?

Me: Wow hooking me up with one day delivery? Sweet!

Amazon: ha-ha yeah man gotta get your book asap!

Me: Ive heard Amazon had great customer service and this just proves it! Thanks man

Amazon: No problem [name], is there any other issue or question that I can help you with?

Me: Nah that was it. Really appreciate it.

Amazon: Anytime bro. Have a great day. Goodbye Odin

Me: Bye my son

***

Almost makes you look forward to a customer service problem with Amazon, doesn't it? People buy from people, not businesses. They also buy from people they know, like, and trust. By being real, you become more than a cold, unapproachable business. You become a trusted friend. And that, my friend, is how you want to be perceived.

It's also the beginning of the next tactic you need to be aware of as a content marketer, building your list. Let's review some smart approaches to list building.

Ted Box

Chapter 5

Growing Your List

Once you have content creation and delivery mastered, your next step is promotion. The easiest way to do this is to grow a list of responsive people who love your brand and your content. Then, when you have a new piece of content, you only need to send them an email with a link to access it.

Easy, right? It is if you have a good list. But let's define "good." When talking about a mailing list, it's important to distinguish size from quality. You can have a huge list and still have a low clickthrough rate and low sales.

That's not worth bragging about. Your goal should be depth and breadth, not sheer numbers.

There are plenty of Internet marketers who brag about their huge lists. And they're eager to give you tactics for getting more people on your list quickly. I'll cover a few of these tactics, but we aren't going to spend a lot of time on them—largely because I question the quality of the prospects they bring in.

In this chapter, I cover the basics of list building and then share some strategies for growing your list with quality subscribers.

List Building 101

Let's return to the issue of list size. Which is more valuable: a list of 500 or of 500,000? The quick answer is 500,000. But what if I told you that the 500,000-person list has a huge bounce rate and a .05 percent clickthrough rate, while the 500-person list has a 23% clickthrough rate? In this case, the smaller list is made up of hyper-responsive prospects and customers, which makes it much higher value than the larger list.

When building your list, you don't simply want to add more people. You want to add the *right* people. A highly responsive list will be made up of qualified prospects and customers. They will be decision makers and have authority to buy. They will also be congruent members of your tribe. Your goal is not to attract competitors, students writing reports, or low-level employees with no influence.

So how do you ensure you build a quality list? Start with your customers. This checklist should help you identify what your ideal customer looks like—so you know who you're targeting when building your list.

Identify your audience or market

- Describe your ideal customer. What specific qualities does he have: demographics, psychographics, hobbies, etc.?
- What information is he looking for that you can share: Tips? Ideas? How to?

Identify your ideal customer

- Build a clear picture in your mind.
- Identify his fears, frustrations and dreams.
- What does he secretly desire?

Identify his content/product needs

- What types of content tends to attract him?
- What format does he prefer: video, audio, text?
- Does he prefer free downloads, or is he willing to pay for information?
- If so, how much is he willing to spend?
- What does he perceive as valuable?

What Are You Willing to Give Away?

Once you've identified your ideal prospect, you need to decide what you're going to give away in return for his email address.

Types of giveaways

Think carefully about what you are willing to give away. Your prospects must feel that they got the better end of this exchange. But you don't want to create unnecessary work on your end. Give away as much value as you can afford, but keep it as simple to create an maintain as possible. Here are a few ideas.

High-value content

Not all content is created equal. Some formats are perceived as higher value than others. These often make your best giveaways because visitors value them so highly.

- Books
- Videos
- Audio
- Excerpts from paid presentations and/or Q&A sessions
- Personal stories
- Training programs

Evergreen content

Evergreen content is information that has a long shelf-life. It is likely to remain useful for years rather than months. Fortunately, it is perceived as valuable by most people, and it makes your life easier, since you don't have to update it frequently.

- FAQs
- Client stories
- Pictures
- Collections from your blog

Breaking-news content

Timely information, which could go out of date soon, is considered high value but needs to be updated or replaced often. If you have time to do that, consider one of these giveaways.

- Comments about or explanation of market trends
- Market data
- Surveys
- Business or industry news

Tools and resources

Useful resources are seen as extremely high value, but they may require frequent updates.

- Software or app
- Product announcement
- Resource lists

Qualities of irresistible giveaways

Whatever the giveaway, it must do three things:

Target an existing problem or challenge. People are most interested in information that helps them solve a pressing problem. That's why it's important to know your audience. If you can create an offer that states the problem in their own words, and offers the exact solution they want, you'll have the perfect giveaway.

Provide an easy or fast solution. People don't want more work. Create a solution that's easy or quick. If it's a copy-and-paste solution or done-for-you, all the better.

Hit emotional hot buttons. It's easy to over-shoot your target. While your giveaway may outline a process for earning $100,000 in 6 months, it could actually miss the prospect whose goal is to earn enough money to quit her job. While it's true that $100,000 would actually meet her goal, the offer is too big, which makes it less credible and less likely to catch her eye as she scans your offer. Use the words your audience is using, and target the precise problem they're trying to solve, and you'll attract more qualified prospects with your giveaway.

Traditional List-Building Tactics

When building your list, you must create an exchange—in most cases, useful information in exchange for an email address. The exchange is made through an opt-in gate, or subscription form.

The key to making this work is to create enough value for your subscribers that they are willing to accept an ongoing relationship with you. The challenge is that this isn't a new strategy and has been abused enough to make your visitors wary. They know that by giving you their email address, they could potentially receive a flood of junk or spam emails. As a result, there has to be a significant amount of trust for them to be willing to make that exchange.

How are opt-in gates used for list building? Here are the most common tactics.

Website: Blog subscription

On most websites that also have a blog, readers are offered the chance to subscribe, so they don't miss a single blog post. As you see, the exchange is fairly low value—your email address in exchange for an email each time the blog publishes.

This is the easiest way to ask for email subscribers—and probably the least effective. That's because readers don't need to subscribe to find your content. In most cases, they can access your articles through their favorite RSS reader, by following you in social media, or simply by visiting your website when the mood strikes them. In other words, they don't have to give you their email in order to access your content.

Website: High-value content

Hoping to up the ante and entice people to subscribe, many businesses offer a unique piece of content—valuable enough to sell, yet offered free in exchange for a visitor's subscription. This content may stand alone, or it may be a gift for subscribing.

This has been a good tactic, but it's been so overused, it is beginning to lose its effectiveness. Consumers don't tend to value gated content as highly when they can get equally high-value content free on many blogs. And they are becoming as jaded about opt-ins as they are about paid products. All too often, the value is highly overrated: After opting in, they get a low-value piece of content and an in-box full of junk emails. Remember, your prospects aren't interested in making a low-value exchange with you. You must offer useful content, and you must convince visitors that you won't abuse their personal information.

In most cases, businesses offer a special report, study, eBook, training course or email sequence. Depending upon your audience, special reports and eBooks may not be the draw they once were. However, free training or an email series are often effective. The key is to offer information your readers want and to make your content as high value as possible.

LinkedIn or Facebook: "Free" giveaways

This is a relatively new strategy being used by social brands, and it's particularly effective since it doesn't immediate look like an email subscription. This tactic takes place off-site, usually in Facebook or LinkedIn.

An ad is shown to people who meet your pre-selected criteria. In it, you offer a free giveaway, usually a checklist, a case study (with instructions) or a how-to piece. Responders are taken to a dedicated landing page, where they can fill out your form to download the giveaway.

The key to this type of promotion is to correctly identify the criteria of your target audience. If done well, you can weed out people who aren't your ideal customers, which means your list is cleaner and more targeted. One tip: Keep your form as streamlined as possible. Too many form fields, and you could make people leery about opting in. Think about how much information you really need at this stage.

Webinar/event: Free attendance

Another way to attract new opt-ins is to offer a free webinar, teleseminar or other high-value event. These events may be live or play-on-demand. They should offer useful content to justify the opt-in. As with the Facebook promotion, you need a landing page to promote the event and collect opt-ins. You can drive traffic to the page through email, social media, and advertising.

Get Traction from Your List-Building Efforts

All of the tactics listed above can work. The LinkedIn/Facebook and Webinar/Event tactics can be especially effective at attracting people who are interested in your products. But they may also attract students and low-level employees who have no purchase authority.

Remember, your ideal list is made up of prospects for your products, people who have the authority to buy. Is it possible to attract more of these people? I believe so, if you tap into the power of new gating technology.

Gating is the practice of requiring opt-in before granting access to your readers. In most cases, an opt-in form is used as the gate. But today, you may also see share gates, which require one or more social shares before access may be granted. Leading content marketers argue over the effectiveness of gating content, but all agree that some form of gating is necessary to build your list.

Going viral

You can often improve your list-building efforts simply by leveraging the viral nature of social channels. Create something that's share-worthy—and invite people to share. Here's how.

For this tactic to work, in addition to an opt-in gate, you must use a share gate. I suggest using one type of gate as an access gate, and the other inside your content, prior to delivering your most valuable tips.

Let's say you use a share gate instead of an opt-in gate, meaning users must share your content before they can access it. Then, since you didn't use an opt-in as your access gate, you can use it inside your content. Perhaps you offer a checklist at the end of your freemium. Users must opt-in to get this checklist. But hopefully, you've already impressed them with the quality of your information, so it's a no-brainer to opt in.

That's the basic strategy, and it can work well as it is. But let's look at how you can make it even more effective, so you can prequalify subscribers while building your list.

Instead of an ordinary opt-in gate, create a two-step share gate. In this case, the freemium isn't accessed by your share, but by a second-level share, which occurs when people on your list share the content with *their* followers. Why implement a two-step share? It forces users to share only with people who are likely to be good prospects, so they can achieve the second-level share more quickly.

Now, be aware, people won't jump through hoops to access your content, and if they perceive any access gate to be difficult, they may refuse to walk through it. You must come up with a tactic that works for you and your prospects. Your goal is to find a way to increase your list with the highest value prospects possible.

List-building in an App With today's tech-savvy consumer, if you have an app, you can leverage it to grow your list, just as you would high-value content.

If you have an existing app, consider upgrading it, adding new features, or fixing usability problems. Then re-launch the app, both to existing and new users. If you don't already have an app, consider creating one. It could be an app that solves a simple problem or gives fans quick access to your content. Whatever it does, it must offer value and functionality that your followers will appreciate.

Here's the process for getting the word out:

1. Create ads, social media posts, blog posts and guest posts to promote the app.
2. Include links that take users to the app's landing page.
3. On the landing page, provide an opt-in form to collect users' names and emails.

4. Confirm the subscription.
5. Give them access to the app.

Your List Building Checklist

1. Review your target market behaviors. Create a strategy to guide your actions and implementation.

2. Determine your list-building objectives. You must determine your overall goals for building the list. Do you want to build a massive list of free subscribers or are you focused on building and cultivating a responsible but smaller list of paying customers?

3. Decide on your primary list-building strategy. Consider identifying and implementing a strategy that involves a giveaway of a free report, an eZine, or a product. If you prefer to build a list of paying customers, forego the free giveaway and provide a high-value product for a low entry price.

4. Decide on your secondary list-building strategy. This could involve a product, program, or specific approaches you wish to implement to build your list. For instance, you may implement a free sign-up for access to a pre-release product or service.

5. Identify opt-in points. Consider your overall list-building strategy and spend time identifying the points where you could place opt-in forms.

6. Create or compile your giveaways.

7. Set up your opt-in pages. For each opt-in point, you need to set up a specific opt-in page to maximize your conversions.

8. Implement sharing. For each opt-in you receive, you can increase exposure to additional prospects if you implement tell-a-friend technology.

9. Set up your newsletter. If you don't already have one, consider setting up a newsletter that is delivered to your subscribers on a consistent basis. If you regularly provide valuable content, a newsletter is an excellent way to develop a relationship with your list.

10. Document your plan. By writing it down, all team members can access it, so there is less confusion about what needs to be done, and by whom. Written plans also tend to help reach completion more easily.

11. Work your plan.

Chapter 6

Advanced Content Strategies

We've covered content creation, content delivery, content improvement, and strategies for building your list. If you implement the strategies I've shared to this point and do nothing else, you're still more advanced than the average content marketer. You are creating magnetic copy, which means you can get people's attention and beat 95% of your competition.

Is that good enough? What if you could beat the other 5%? You can, if you're willing to invest some brain power to take your content to yet another level.

Up to this point, we've largely talked about the need for magnetic content. Using that image, let's see how we can create *electro*magnetic content. Cheesy? Perhaps. But you need to be willing to go to all lengths to engage your audience and drive action. Otherwise, what's the point?

Your challenge, as a content marketer, is to create engagement beyond that which the average business achieves. Most brands publish content and average a one- or two-percent open rate. Who knows whether the content is being read and acted on? The marketing team dusts off their hands and congratulates themselves on a job well done. The project was completed on time, and it looked good. People are downloading, so the project is a success.

Um. No. That's neither a job well done, nor a success. Marketing is a science as well as an art. A good looking piece of content isn't enough. You need to measure engagement levels and figure out how to improve results.

The Formula for Next-Level Content

I'd like to share a formula that could get you thinking. You've seen it before:

$$E = mc^2$$

Kinetic energy (e) equals mass times the speed of light, squared. The Theory of Relativity, as developed by Albert Einstein.

What does it have to do with content marketing? The concept of relativity has little to do with our work. But energy is central to content marketing. Think about it. We weave ideas and words together to promote a business, a product, or an idea. Through it, we tell stories, tickle people's imagination, inspire them, challenge them, and persuade them to act. Not in some vague, imprecise way, but in the way we want, in a way that's most beneficial (and profitable) to us. We're marketers. Like it or not, we're in the business of influencing people.

Our job requires energy. Kinetic energy, if you will. If I look it up, Google tells me that the kinetic energy of an object is "the energy that it possesses due to its motion. It is defined as the work needed to accelerate a body of a given mass from rest to its stated velocity."

Kinetic energy takes a body at rest and gives it the push it needs to start moving. It's transfers action from one body to another. But to do that, the energy of Body #1 must be sufficient to share. (Simplistic, I know, but it makes the point.)

This is why most marketing doesn't get results. It lacks energy. And I have a few guesses as to why.

First, the original copy may not have been written by a skilled writer. Bad copy is often bad because it lacks energy. There's no fix for this. You need a better copywriter.

Second, assuming you have good copy—written by an experienced writer who has injected it with energy—it can be edited to death, all the life sucked out of it by endless rounds of editing. It happens, and you know it. Adequate copy ends up being unusable after everyone has taken a round with Track Edits. Even if the writer smooths out the rough edges, the copy remains lifeless. The words may be right, the ideas on track, but the original energy is now gone.

This is the copy most marketing departments publish. Not to blame them. Their job is to publish approved branding statements, no matter how little energy they contain. By publishing gobbledygook, they're simply doing what they were hired to do.

Let's assume we can put an end death-by-editing. In a perfect world, you could create high-energy content, tweak the message without killing it altogether, and publish something worth reading. What's the difference between fresh content that sparkles with personality and unique ideas?

In a word, *energy*. To be more specific, *kinetic energy*.

To take your content to the highest level, you must be allowed to inject it with kinetic energy. This is the energy that makes people take notice. It's the big idea, the original turn of phrase, the unique way of looking at a topic, the subtle word play that never draws attention to itself but makes word nerds smile. It does all this "writerly" stuff without ever sacrificing the underlying sales agenda. And again, it's so subtle, your readers aren't turned off. They're energized and can't wait to take action.

You've seen this, I'm sure.

Harley Davidson has such an energetic brand, people tattoo themselves with it. Coca-Cola's *The Real Thing*, created a line in the sand. Even if a taste challenge failed, the energy of the brand won out; fans refuse to drink any other cola. In these cases, the energy comes from the brand itself, as well as the content.

But content is the perfect way to generate and share that energy. Dan Kennedy does this with his *No B.S.* style of communication. His target audience, entrepreneurs and small business owners, read everything he writes. It's like diesel fuel in their tanks, and keeps them going until the next piece of content arrives.

This is the gold standard. And the secret is in the formula.

Kinetic energy, in content marketing, translates into engagement. But engagement can't be achieved if you think about it as the catchphrase we talk about in marketing circles. The word has been bandied about so much, it has almost lost its meaning. Is it readership? Is it sharability? Is it fan bait? In reality engagement is all three. It is content that's so full of energy, people can't pass it up. If they don't have time to read it now, they save it and make time to come back. But they *do* come back. It's that magnetic.

Engaging content attracts your target market, compels them to click through, to open, and consume. It entertains them while informing them. And it does it so well, they're eager to share it.

This kinetic quality is key. The content (body #1) contains kinetic energy. It transfers that energy to readers (body #2). And that exchange drives action.

Now, let's look at the equation again.

$$E = mc^2$$

Kinetic energy, or engagement is created by magnetic content (repeated). What does that mean? It means this type of energy is difficult to achieve on the first try. You must adopt a content improvement cycle, and you must allow content creators to test ideas for exponential engagement.

Remember, the processes and systems that you have always used will only get the results you've always had. For next-level content marketing, you must adopt a culture of testing. Testing new ideas. Testing new ways of saying things. Testing new content delivery styles and formats. And testing new technology within your content. The content contains not just text, but motion and sound as well. The content doesn't just deliver your message, but also allows readers to respond.

Bigger brands will have a harder time with this than small ones because in medium to large businesses, the brand is god. You have only three things you can say about your product, and you can only say them with a particular set of words. Sorry. I just heard your content roll over and die. May it rest in peace.

Next-level content requires more. More daring. More flexibility. More everything. You need balls, my friend. You must be willing to cut your knee or fall through a crevice as you make your way up the mountain. But I promise you, the trek is worth it. At the peak, after you've navigated the obstacles and created a message that perfectly resonates with your audience, your content shines. *This* is highest level content marketing. It is content infused with kinetic energy. And this is the goal.

Fair warning: This isn't the type of content you write in an hour and post on your blog. It isn't your thoughts dropped quickly from the keyboard. Electromagnetic content gets under people's skin and stays with them. It's not what you want to tell them; it's what they want to hear.

What they want to hear

True success with content marketing comes when you find the intersection between what you want to say and what they want to hear.

You have to get inside the mind of your audience. You have to be able to create a message that perfectly aligns with the monologues going on inside their heads. So it isn't just about offering benefits, but about solving the worry or fear that's gnawing at them.

That's the source of energy in electromagnetic content. And it's why it successfully attracts your best prospects. We've talked extensively about how to create next-level content. Magnetic content is the highest quality. It stands out from the pack. It resonates with your audience. So how do you do that?

First, you must know who you are talking to. Not just who they are, but what their qualities are, the challenges they face, their fears and worries. Not just their role in life, but their hobbies, the brands they follow on Facebook, their favorite television shows.

Second, you need to know how they perceive you. Are you their guide into a strange, new land? Are you a buddy, just like them, sharing your journey with them? Or are you an elite guru, coming down from your cave to share your superhuman wisdom? Your own persona directs the style and format of your content.

And finally, you need to know what *exactly* you sell. Weird question, I know. But stay with me. Let's look at a few great brands to see what they sell.

- Subway: Not sandwiches. Weight loss. (Remember the Jarod commercials?)
- Starbucks: Not coffee. A coffee break in a stylish environment.
- Coca-Cola: Not a soft drink. Happiness.
- Harley Davidson: Not motorcycles. Freedom from the constraints of life.

You see, what you sell is isn't a product. That could be perceived as a commodity. You sell an experience or an idea. So it's critical that you fully understand what you offer your customers—if you want to be a next-level content marketer. You do that by defining your sales moment and creating a powerful brand.

Ready to dive deep into some brain-rattling marketing training? Let's go.

Define Your Sales Moment

The Sales Moment is the one thing that can be said of your company's products or services that actually attracts your best prospects and converts them into paying customers. It's the deep promise (the energy) that resonates with your prospects. Your brand must communicate this moment, and it does so through four branding elements. If you fail, the brand is weak and will confuse people. If you succeed, you generate kinetic energy that magnetically attracts your best prospects.

The sales moment occurs at the moment that your brand promise connects with your prospects' desire. It is the spark that occurs when the light bulb goes off and your prospects realize they *must* have your product. In essence, it's the moment when they convert mentally into customers before buying.

Where do you find it? At the intersection of your brand's strengths, your customers' desires, and your competitors' weakness.

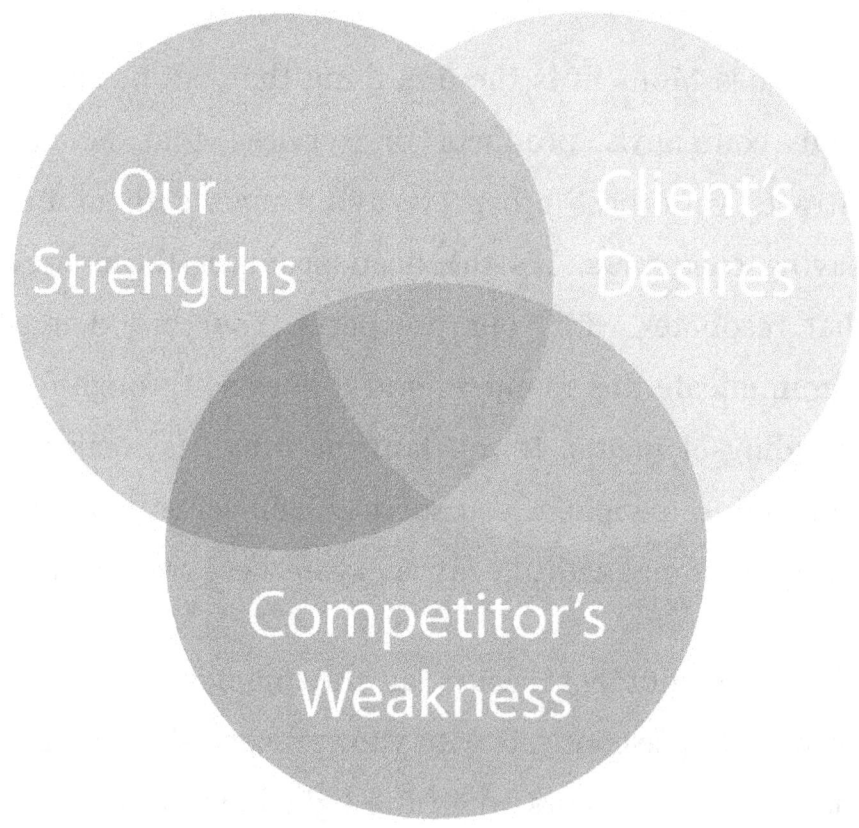

This is where you'll find the white space, the exact place where you can provide for a need that no one else can fill. If you can communicate it clearly and quickly, it can deliver the aha! moment that creates instant desire.

Generally, you can tell which companies haven't defined their sales moment. Their brochures have no congruent theme, no consistent branding. The ad may be effective, but the landing page that's tied to it doesn't seem to fit.

A company that has defined its sales moment has a consistent look and feel and a congruent message across platforms. They have a singular value statement that connects with their best prospects and drives everything they do. And it is an integral part of the brand itself.

Branding

The term *brand* is one of the more overused and most misunderstood terms in marketing. Let's see if I can tap into some memories of how my esteemed colleague, James Connor, would have addressed this topic.

Three levels of branding

The first level of branding has to do with your identity. In this case, branding is used as an identifier of the company, its goods and services. Think of Nike Oedipus, the ancient Greek shoe maker, taking a hot iron to stamp his mark on the sandals he produced by hand.

The second level of branding has to do with your promise of a unique customer experience. Since my shampoo comes from Johnson & Johnson, I know it is safe to use. It wasn't mixed in some trough by a disreputable company, potentially causing my hair to fall out. J&J promises manageable hair, and I trust them. Starbucks offers a similar promise. I can enter any of their coffee houses anywhere in the world and know what to expect. That is a promise of customer experience.

The third level of branding is the most subtle—and also the most powerful. It's the single idea owned by a company that tilts sales in its favor. For example, if I say "family fast food," the odds are pretty good that you are going to think of McDonalds. What if I said "family entertainment"? Your thoughts might move towards Disney. If I were to say "the fizzy drink that makes you smile," many people think of Coke, given their campaigns focused on putting a smile on your face. But owning a brand position is not absolute. When prompted by "fizzy drink," some people will think of a cocktail rather than Coke.

Think about the single idea that your company needs to own in order to tilt sales in your favor. Not as easy as it sounds, is it? That's because, as marketers, we tend to think tactically. Our sole interest tends to be task-based, like building a website, creating a brochure, saying *this* or *that* in an email. Uncovering the single idea that captures a brand often requires you to return to the basics, to focusing on your brand.

Creating your brand

Most people think of a brand as a color palette and a set of fonts. But in actuality, a brand is a sellable idea, owned by you and resonating with your customers. Without this sellable idea, you can run a profitable business. You can even develop good name recognition. But if you want to become an icon in your industry, this is the missing link. Brands like Apple, Disney, and McDonalds are top companies for just this reason.

Now, as we talk about branding, don't imagine for a moment that we've strayed from content marketing. As a content creator, you have to create content that stands out from the clutter and captures people's attention. How easy is it to do your job if you have a secondary, or worse, an unrecognizable, brand? People see an announcement from you, and they don't care. Meanwhile, the Disney of your industry makes a similar piece of content, and everyone raves.

Branding does matter to content marketers. Especially for us, the brand is the strongest asset. Get this right and content creation becomes easier. Your name alone attracts attention. Then, because you've done the work to refine a single idea that communicates your essence, writing is easier. Engagement is easier. *Everything* is easier.

Power branding isn't for big companies only. Every company (yes, even yours) has the power to create a brand that resonates. You simply have to uncover that single idea that communicates what you stand for and how it makes things easier for your customers. The key is communicating it well, so people can easily see how you fit into their world.

4 elements of a power brand

The four major elements of a powerful brand are Name, Logo, Tagline, and Ad Campaign

From a potential customer's perspective these four elements are experienced simultaneously, and they are so integrated, it's often hard to separate them. All four of these elements must quickly create a mental image that communicates the sales moment.

Let's look at each in depth.

1. Name

When you create a brand, the name *must* help to create a mental image based on verbal cues. There are six different types of names used by the most successful brands of all time. Each of the types helps the brand achieve a particular objective and at the same time communicate the sales moment.

Think about the idea that your company is trying to *own,* and how you might own it more effectively with the right name.

Creating a powerful brand name begins with understanding the different naming types: function, metaphor, energy, morpheme, historic, and family.

Function

- Liquid Plumber
- Toys R Us
- ThinkFun

If you select a functional name, be careful with the other brand elements (logo, tagline, ad image, etc.) so the company does not appear cheap or unsophisticated compared to other brands. Functional names use a key product feature that you want to own.

Metaphor

- TransparentValue (an asset management company)
- Amazon (name conveys size)

The focus here is on creating strategic value using a word that suggests a desirable quality of your brand.

Energy

- Big Ass Fans (yes, that is the company name)
- OshKosh B'Gosh (it's just fun to say, especially for the target market, toddlers)

Energy naming uses words that convey an emotion, action, or tone associated with the brand to achieve effect.

Morpheme

- Microsoft
- Verizon
- FedEx

A morpheme is the smallest grammatical unit in a language. In branding, morphemes use small syllables of a word or words to convey essential meaning. These syllables can be combined to form a new word like FedEx (from Federal Express) and Microsoft.

Historic

- Rembrandt toothpaste
- Baby Einstein
- Con Edison

Historic naming uses an historic event, character or location to embody a brand.

Family

- McDonalds
- Ford
- Samsung

Family naming uses either real or fictional names, usually from the founders, to convey the sales moment effectively. This is especially useful when you need to differentiate your brand from the competition.

Once you have a clear brand idea to work with, develop names using all six approaches. Then you can determine which type of naming works best to convey the sales moment and helps you to own your brand idea. Then do trademark searches on the best names to see which are available. Choose the name that is the most memorable and best expresses your strategic idea.

Caution: Do *not* select a company name that you like the best or one that others like the best. You may not like your company name at all, but that doesn't matter. The names that historically succeed are the ones that are most memorable, that best express their sales moment.

A few more tips: Avoid names that are challenging to spell or difficult to pronounce easily. Do some research and drop names that have negative connotations in languages that are important to your market.

2. Logo

Simplicity is the key to a great logo, as long as it is memorable. Customers need to be able to construct the logo easily in their mind so that they have a clear and unique mental image of your brand.

The stronger your mental image, the more likely they are to remember you. Successful logos are simple in a symbolic way, memorable, differentiated from the competition, and tell a story. The story must be closely related to your sales moment.

In addition, the logo must support the mental image created by your brand. Be sure that your logo is different from those used by your competitors.

3. Tagline

Great taglines bring a brand to life. They should NOT include a description of your products or services. Great taglines communicate why your brand is relevant to your target customers by calling up the sales moment. There are 3 types of taglines:

- Promises
- Calls to Action
- Memory taglines

Promises are based on a key brand attribute. Calls to action are invitations for prospects to join your community because they share similar philosophies. Memory taglines play off the names or logos to help people remember the brands.

Examples:

- Timex – It takes a licking and keeps on ticking (promise)
- Apple – Think different (call to action)
- Army – Be all you can be (call to action)
- Maybelline – Maybe she's born with it. Maybe it's Maybelline? (memory)
- Prudential – Own a piece of the rock (memory)

- Duracell – You can't top the copper top (promise & memory)

Here's another angle on creating killer taglines that I think you will enjoy. The following taglines all have a few things in common. They focus on the user experience (the UX), offer eye-opening comparisons, and come from highly memorable brands. My guess is that these brands are memorable because of their superb taglines.

- ClubMed – The antidote for civilization
- GLAD – Don't get mad, get GLAD.
- Memorex – Is it live or is it Memorex?
- Outback Steakhouse – No rules. Just right.
- Secret Deodorant – Strong enough for a man, but made for a woman
- Target – Expect more. Pay less.
- United Negro College Fund – The mind is a terrible thing to waste.
- US Marines – We're looking for a few good men.

- MasterCard – There are some things that money can't buy. For everything else there's MasterCard.

If you're in the United States and are over 30, there's a good chance you recognize all of these tag lines. What's more, I'll bet you can even envision how the advertising looked and sounded. A good tag line makes your brand memorable.

Below are a few more. These companies have powerful ad agencies and multi-million dollar branding budgets yet, how many of the following brands' taglines do you remember? Each of the following taglines relates to their product or service, not the user experience.

- Ernst & Young – Quality in everything we do
- Fancy Feast – Good taste is easy to recognize
- Ford – Bold Moves
- Honda – The power of dreams
- Pepsi – For those who think young
- Wells Fargo – The next stage
- Aflac – Ask about it at work

- Bank of America – Higher standards
- Cheez-It – Get your own box
- CNET – The source for computing and technology

Does your tagline quickly explain why your brand is relevant to your target customer and, at the same time, differentiate you from your competitors?

Tip: wrap your tagline around the desired user experience and compare or contrast it with something your target customers want or don't want to experience.

4. Ad Campaign

In the history of the world, there have been only four "hooks" for advertising campaigns that build brands and drive sales. These hooks are a word, a character, a theme, or a layout.

Word: repeatable word or catch phrase, which becomes the hook for each ad.

- Verizon – Can you hear me now?
- MasterCard – priceless

Character hook: the character may be a hero, hero, or villain. There's just one challenge with this type of campaign. People may not remember the brand that goes with the character.

- McDonald's – Ronald McDonald. Only Santa Clause is more recognizable than Ronald McDonald.
- Dos Equis – the most interesting man in the world. He's always in a unique situation, always challenging us to stay thirsty. Notice how well the tag line connects with the hook in this case.
- Morris the Cat – Which brand was that? I can't remember! Always make sure your character easily relates to your brand name. That's why Ronald McDonald and Geico's gecko have been so successful.

Repeatable theme: a situation that happens again and again creating a need for the product, or the same situation (joke) is played out again and again.

- Citibank – live richly
- Reese's Peanut Butter Cups – You got your peanut butter on my chocolate bar!

Consistent layout: a unique look and feel that is easily identifiable.

- Apple – Zen, white. A cool silhouette with colorful people against a white background. The tag, think different, is always communicated.
- National Geographic – their gold box, which rims their iconic magazines, is now their logo.

Powerful branding and content marketing

For content creators, nothing is more limiting that a brand, especially if it also comes with an enforcer, who is overly rigid. The best content often happens when the content creator (writer or artist) makes a mental leap that creates a new way to communicate the brand message within its guidelines. You must allow for this. A brand needs breathing room if it's going to stay current and continue to resonate with your audience.

Even if you have a solid, successful brand, you must allow your creative team the ability to create. Otherwise, why use them? If your brand consists of exact phrases that must be repeated again and again, your content is already dry, brittle and lifeless. No amount of creative execution will resurrect it, and no advertising genius will make it better.

If you allow your brand to be a tyrant, fire your writers and hire some extra programmers. Plug in your pet phrases and get on with business. But don't complain that engagement is low. That's what happens when your brand can't flex its muscles and express itself creatively in your content.

Let's move on. As you can see, your brand is the unique expression of who you are and how you can make your customers' lives easier. It captures the idea of how you fit into your customers' lives, who they become when they are part of your ecosystem (think Harley Davidson and Apple). It also helps you define your sales moment.

Understanding the Buying Journey

Marketing basically has one goal: to reach prospects at those key moments that most influence their decisions. To do that, it's imperative that you understand the decision path that buyers travel on their way to a purchase.

Marketing has always sought those moments, or touch points, when consumers are open to influence. For years, we've made those touches in a particular framework, known as the sales funnel. At the top of the funnel are many prospects, all of them unqualified, most of them researching or reviewing their options. The deeper into the funnel you go, the fewer prospects remain until, at the bottom of the funnel, there are only qualified, warm prospects, most of whom are ready to buy.

The progression matches the buyer's journey: awareness, familiarity, consideration, purchase, loyalty. And our job is to create distinct and separate touch points, through which we weed out the folks who aren't good prospects for our products and nurture those who are.

Content is one of the most powerful ways to attract prospects to your funnel. In most cases, they are researching a problem, looking for options. If your brand has blog articles or other high-value content relating to their search, you will show up in search engines. You are then more likely to be one of the brands that makes it into the initial consideration set as your prospects begin their buying journey.

How consumers make decisions

We tend to like the funnel as an image of the buying journey because it is linear, which makes it easy to visualize. We feel confident that the right message at the right time will push people through the funnel towards the ultimate sale.

But according to a McKinsey study, this isn't an accurate image. They believe the decision-making process is circular, rather than linear, with four phases providing yet another area where you can win or lose:

1. Initial consideration, in which they select a handful of possibilities that appear to be a good fit.

2. Active evaluation, when they compare your product against others in their consideration set.

3. Closure, when they make their decision and buy.

4. Post-purchase, when they experience the product and compare its reality to the marketing messages that made them buy.

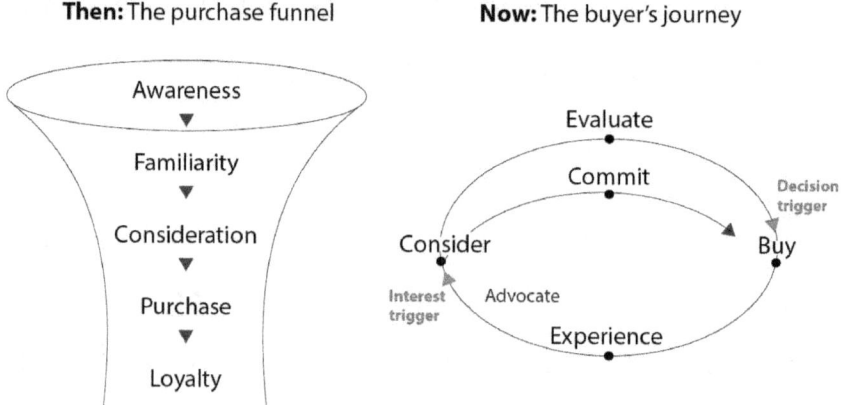

Brand consideration

The challenge for marketers is the global marketplace, which gives consumers hundreds, if not thousands, of choices for nearly every purchase they make. The challenge for consumers is the same. Research has shown that too much choice actually makes it harder to choose. Given the immense number of choices consumers face, it's amazing they are able to progress towards purchase at all!

Their solution is to be highly selective about which brands make it into their consideration set. Consumers tend to fall back on the limited set of brands that they already know and, therefore, already trust. They also rely on recommendations from friends.

As you can see, brand awareness matters. In fact, according to McKinsey, if you're in this initial consideration set, you are three times more likely to be purchased eventually than if you aren't.

This is why content is king. In an attention economy, the brand that has already earned consumer awareness makes it into the consideration pool. If it is liked by the consumer, it's even more likely to win consideration.

Empowered consumers

When designing our content, we tend to think in terms of touch points. We try to create attention-getting touches for the top of the funnel and relationship-building touches deeper in the funnel. This stems from a well-ingrained tradition of push marketing.

But marketing is no longer a one-way, push-style process. Through social media and word of mouth, consumers continually add their opinions to your message. Through the Internet, they can actively pull information at will from your website and social channels. This dramatically changes the concept of a touch point.

Research has shown that two-thirds of the touches made during the active-evaluation period are initiated by the consumer. Only a third of the touch points are company-driven marketing. Clearly, we need to be sure we're providing information that meets these early consumer-led inquiries. We need to be focusing, not just on content creation or sales, but on brand awareness, brand perception, and relationship.

Two types of loyalty

After you make an expensive purchase, do you stop reviewing your options? For most consumers (60%), the buying journey doesn't end with purchase. That's why it's so important to include post-purchase touch points that reassure the customer that he's made a good decision and deepen his loyalty to your brand.

This is important for two reasons. First, loyal customers (those who are happy with their choice) may recommend you to their friends, increasing the likelihood that you'll make it into more people's consideration sets. Second, passive loyal customer (new customers who are unsure of their choice) may see something better and switch to a competitor. In fact, some brands (think GEICO and Progressive) actually build campaigns designed to win passively loyal customers of other companies.

The lesson is clear. You not only need content that wins attention and builds relationship. You also need content that turns passively loyal customers into actively loyal customers, people who are willing to evangelize your brand and share it with their connections.

Aligning content with the consumer decision journey

At every stage of the buying journey, your prospects have questions. While it seems logical to create content for each stage of the journey, an easier, more practical approach is to create content that answers questions.

To do this, you must first develop a deep knowledge of your best prospects. What issues are they concerned with? What problems are they trying to solve? What worries and stresses are they dealing with, and how are they trying to alleviate those stressors? In addition to knowing your customers, you must also understand how your product intersects with their lives. How will they use it? How will it benefit them? And most importantly, what motivates them to buy it?

Once you know your prospects, you understand the content they need at each stage of the buying journey. But beware. It's tempting to create a few pieces that address multiple issues, such as FAQ pages. Next-level content is specific and has a narrow focus. Follow the Rule of One: one piece of content, one question, one solution.

This gives your prospects a reason to continually interact with you. It also builds trust. You see, most of your competitors are going to take the hamster-wheel approach to marketing. They'll create content for stages in the funnel, or they'll create one FAQ piece that's supposed to answer all questions. You, on the other hand, will create unique pieces of content that are dedicated to each individual question your prospects ask.

Now, imagine a consumer moving through his buyer's journey. He has a question and keys it into his favorite search engine. Up comes your content, because it is specific and relevant to his search. A few days later, he has another question, and then another. And each time he does an online search, your brand comes up with a piece of content that directly addresses his question.

If that happens once, you may make it into the consideration set. If it happens three, four, or more times, you will likely win serious evaluation. Why? Because you have demonstrated that you are there for him. And if you are there for him before the sale, he assumes you will also be accessible after the sale.

Using Content to Drive Sales

Content itself should never be a sales medium. In most cases, content is an attention-getting, relationship-building, information-giving medium. But if technology is available, you can still leverage people's interest by including triggers for the sales moment.

In blog posts, for example, you might place an action box, promoting a product related to the topic you're talking about. Or in your call to action, you might offer more information, and have a link take readers to another, more in-depth piece of content or a sales page.

In eBooks or brochures, think beyond the call to action. Consider including share gates, opt-in gates, popups and other methods for the engaged readers to take the action you're driving. In addition, try to be more creative with your gates.

To gate or not to gate

For years, the traditional list-building technique has been an opt-in gate leading to high-value content, such as a special report or eBook. Content purists, however, tend to disagree with this tactic. They say content should be free for anyone to download and read; otherwise, why create it. Their approach tends to get more downloads and more name recognition, but it fails to generate leads or build a list.

If you evaluate their approach to marketing, they are essentially saying that we have to add value before asking for anything in return—a position that I support completely. But they are assuming that there is no other option than an access gate before download.

Today, technology exists that allows you to add value *before* asking for the opt-in. The gate can be placed inside your content, say, before you give a final checklist or your best tip. If your content has been useful up to that point, it's less objectionable to opt in.

In addition, you can use one of two types of gates. In many cases, you need to build your list, in which case the traditional opt-in gate is appropriate. But in some cases, you may simply want to extend your reach. In this case, a share gate may meet your goals better.

Conclusion: The Key is Engagement

Bottom line, you need eyeballs on your message—but not anyone's eyeballs; you need the eyes of your best prospects. Once you've achieved that, you can share your message and drive action. Otherwise, you're shouting to the wind.

The key is engagement. But as you've seen in this book, engagement is much more than excitement, hype, or overblown stories. It has to do with knowing your audience and crafting a message that resonates with them.

Ultimately, there are two ways to engage your audience: through the content itself and your delivery, which can include the platform as well as the format. Every element of your content and delivery must be impressive. It must be relevant. And it must capture and convey the kinetic energy that makes your brand resonate with your best prospects.

When each of these elements is in place, you become, not just a content creator, but a next-level content marketer, a master of engagement.

10 Steps to Next-Level Content Marketing

1. Get to know your target audience. Really know them.

2. Find your Sales Moment, the sweet spot of your strengths, your competitors' weaknesses, and your audience's desires.

3. Develop a brand and a core message that are nestled in that sweet spot.

4. Find the questions your audience asks at every stage of the buying journey.

5. Create magnetic content that answers those questions.

6. Select a delivery platform and format that is as magnetic as your content.

7. Be generous with your knowledge, and generous with your content.

8. Find new ways to leverage technology to allow readers to respond at the exact moment they want more information.

9. Become a numbers person—always track results.

10. Create a cycle of improvement. Implement content optimization to constantly improve your engagement and response levels.

The Credo of Next-Level Content Creators

As content marketers, we have a mission. We must craft a message that resonates with our audience while remaining faithful to our brand and sales mission. It's a bigger challenge than most people realize. But we are the creative in this business world. Let's agree to hold ourselves to a higher standard.

I leave you with a challenge. Stop settling for hamster-wheel content marketing. Don't just create content for the sake of content. Step up your efforts and take your content to the next level.

This credo is only for next-level content marketers. I challenge you to make it your own.

"I will not create content for content's sake. I will invest the time and energy to create content worth reading and worth sharing. I commit to my audience that I will not bore them with marketing blather, but entertain, educate and enlighten them. And I will always strive to create a win-win scenario, where my own business needs and the needs of my audience are equally met."

Go forth, my friend, and create content worth talking about.

184   Ted Box

Appendix

Ted Box

Resources

KinetiZine™

www.KinetiZine.com

A content delivery format that allows you to use the same functionality available on a website in your content. So you can create hotspots, workflows, share gates or opt-in gates. You can get analytics and even create automatic work flows based on user behavior.

TabletPublisherPro

www.TabletPublisherPro.com

Publish your content as an app. Full-service consultation and app creation.

Killian Branding

www.killianbranding.com

Branding agency. Company naming, renaming, marketing, social media, design, digital, KinetiZines™.

AAAA. Chicago. Advertising. Creative, strategic finch watchers adapting, evolving since 1987.

Notes

Cialdini, Robert B. Yes! 50 Scientifically Proven Ways to Be Persuasive. New York: Free Press, 2008.

Court, David; Dave Elzinga; Susan Mulder; and Ole Jørgen Vetvik. McKinsey & Company. The McKinsey Quarterly. "The Consumer Decision Journey." http://www.mckinsey.com/insights/marketing_sales/the_consumer_decision_journey. June 2009.

Gabbert, Elisa. "The Attention Economy: Why Some of Your Content Will Always Fail." http://www.wordstream.com/blog/ws/2014/05/23/attention-economy#. May 23, 2014.

Gallup Consulting. The Next Discipline: Applying Behavioral Economics to Drive Growth and Profitability. http://www.gallup.com/strategicconsulting/122906/next-discipline.aspx.

Gates, Bill. "Content Is King." http://www.craigbailey.net/content-is-king-by-bill-gates/ Copyright of the essay is held by Microsoft, 2001. The blog post is by Craig Bailey. May 31, 2010.

Goldhaber, Michael H. "Attention Shoppers!" http://archive.wired.com/wired/archive/5.12/es_attention.html. December 1997.

Havas Worldwide. "Study Highlights" from a study on The New Consumer. http://www.thenewconsumer.com/study-highlights/

Hogshead, Sally. Fascinate: Your 7 Triggers to Persuasion and Captivation. New York: HarperBusiness, 2010.

O'Reilly, Terry and Mike Tennant. The Age of Persuasion. Berkeley, CA: Counterpoint Press, 2009.

Perelman, Jonathan. "Content Is King, But Distribution Is Queen." http://99u.com/videos/23015/jonathan-perelman-content-is-king-distribution-is-queen

Rooney, Jennifer. "Annual Effies Survey: Content Is King." http://www.forbes.com/sites/jenniferrooney/2014/04/16/annual-effies-survey-content-is-king/ April 16, 2014.

Teixeira, Thales; Michel Wedel; and Rik Pieters. Emotion-Induced Engagement in Internet Video Ads. August 2010. http://www.tobii.com/Global/Analysis/Marketing/Research%20Paper/Marketing%20and%20media/EMOTION-INDUCED%20ENGAGEMENT%20IN%20INTERNET%20VIDEO%20ADS.pdf.

Walker, Jeff. The Product Launch Formula. http://jeffwalker.com/

Ted Box

About the Author

Ted Box is a #1 international best-selling author in addition to being the founder and CEO of BoxOnline, a Swiss-based incubator for startup technology ventures that was  established in 1999 to help solve sales and marketing problems for some of the largest brands in the world.

For more than 25 years, Ted has led teams on the cutting edge of software development, delivering sales and marketing success for firms such as AT&T, BroadVision, Tumbleweed, The Swiss Post, Virgin Group, WPP, FindWhat, Yahoo!, Fantastic Corp., Micrognosis, Swisscom, Thomson Reuters, DuPont, Porsche, IBM and dozens more.

Ted often says he learned marketing from some of the best in the world, and it all started with analytics. When he founded BoxOnline, his goal was to help businesses solve marketing problems at scale. Today, he continues on that journey, helping organizations improve their marketing ROI.

"Interrupting people with ads is no longer an option for marketers. It just doesn't work. Our audience expects to be treated with respect. Marketing should be about getting people to know, like and trust you while you provide them with something they value. We firmly believe in creating software that facilitates this objective."

Ted often speaks at conferences on a range of topics:

- The Connection Age (Say Goodbye to Industrial Age Broadcast Tactics)

- Funnel Accelerator (Accelerating Your Sales Funnel)

- Digital Content Distribution (5 reasons why you need to replace your PDFs)

- Boost Your Marketing ROI in 90 days

- 3 Ways To Make Inbound Work For Your Business.

He addresses the evolution of digital marketing, traffic generation methods, the social Web and issues influencing the effectiveness of MARCOM. Ted also conducts best-practice workshops for leading marketers and lectures at the ZfU International Business School in Switzerland.

When he is not solving compelling marketing puzzles, Ted is out sculling, hiking, scuba diving, snowboarding or composing music and doing his best to keep up with the ever-evolving world of tech.

www.ingramcontent.com/pod-product-compliance
Lightning Source LLC
Chambersburg PA
CBHW071419170526
45165CB00001B/331